FINDER
SHORTCUTS ▲

Keyboard Shortcut	Action
⌘-drag window by title bar	Moves window without making it active
Option-double-click item	Closes window while opening selected item within it
Option-drag item	Copies item to desktop or another folder on the same disk instead of moving it
Arrow key	Selects next item in that direction
Tab key	Selects next item in alphabetical order
Letter key	Selects first item whose name starts with that character or next character in the alphabet
Shift-Tab	Selects previous item in alphabetical order
~ (tilde)	Selects the last file in the window

Books that Work Just Like Your Mac

As a Macintosh user, you enjoy unique advantages. You enjoy a dynamic user environment. You enjoy the successful integration of graphics, sound, and text. Above all, you enjoy a computer that's fun and easy to use.

When your computer gives you all this, why accept less in your computer books?

At SYBEX, we don't believe you should. That's why we've committed ourselves to publishing the highest quality computer books for Macintosh users. Externally, our books emulate the Mac "look and feel," with powerful, appealing illustrations and easy-to-read pages. Internally, our books stress "why" over "how," so you'll learn concepts, not sequences of steps. Philosophically, our books are designed to help you get work done, not to teach you about computers.

In short, our books are fun and easy to use—just like the Mac. We hope you find them just as enjoyable.

For a complete catalog of our publications:

SYBEX, Inc.
2021 Challenger Drive, Alameda, CA 94501
Tel: (510) 523-8233/(800) 227-2346 Telex: 336311
Fax: (510) 523-2373

MACINTOSH SYSTEM 7
AT YOUR FINGERTIPS

▲

MACINTOSH®SYSTEM 7 AT YOUR FINGERTIPS ▲

Nancy Dannenberg

SYBEX ®

San Francisco ▲ Paris ▲ Düsseldorf ▲ Soest

Acquisitions Editor: Dianne King
Developmental Editor: Kenyon Brown
Editor: David Krassner
Technical Editor: Celia Stevenson
Word Processors: Ann Dunn and Susan Trybull
Book Designer and Chapter Art: Ingrid Owen
Screen Graphics: Cuong Le
Typesetter: Dina F. Quan
Proofreader: David Avilla Silva
Indexer: Ted Laux
Cover Designer: Ingalls + Associates
Cover Illustrator: Harumi Kubo

Library of Congress Card Number: 91-67559
ISBN: 0-7821-1001-0

Manufactured in the United States of America
10 9 8 7 6 5 4 3 2 1

To a lovely young man, my son Jason

ACKNOWLEDGMENTS

I would like to thank the following individuals for their efforts: Dianne King, acquisitions editor; Kenyon Brown, developmental editor; David Krassner, editor; Celia Stevenson, technical editor; Ann Dunn and Susan Trybull, word processors; Ingrid Owen, book designer and chapter artist; Cuong Le, screen graphics specialist; Dina Quan, typesetter; David Silva, proofreader; and Ted Laux, indexer.

CONTENTS AT A GLANCE

CONTENTS

PART III

PART IV

The Control Panels   90

PART V

The Finder   140

PART VI

PREFACE

If you don't have the time to sit down and plow through some weighty tome to find out how to install and make use of System 7's new features, *Macintosh System 7 at Your Fingertips* is the perfect book for you. You will find this book useful whether you are an experienced user, or have never used a Mac before. You'll find just what you need to know, and no more. Further, this book makes it easy to find exactly what you need.

HOW THIS BOOK IS ORGANIZED

Macintosh System 7 at your Fingertips is organized into six parts.

Part I introduces you to the Mac, stepping you through the basics. Learn how to use the mouse and manipulate windows. Read about renaming, copying, moving, opening, and discarding files and folders from the Finder.

Part II gives you detailed information on installing System 7. Since System 7 might be incompatible with certain applications, installation requires some thought.

Part III tells you about the new System Folder. True-Type fonts, the new System Folder organization, and the expanded role of the Apple Menu Items folder are some of the features described. You don't have to be a power user to make good use of this information.

Part IV describes the control panels. Some are new, some have been changed, and some will be familiar. Read this information to find out how to adjust your Mac so it functions just the way you want it to.

Part V takes you through each of the Finder menus, describing the commands on them. You'll find the new *Publish* and *Subscribe* features described in this section of the book.

Part VI tells you about System 7's built-in file sharing capabilities. Once your computer is physically connected to the network, you can read this section to find out how to make your information available to the network and connect to other user's shared items.

CONVENTIONS IN
THIS BOOK ▲

To guide you quickly to important procedures, notes, related material, and keyboard shortcuts, this book uses repeating icons, which look like this:

PROCEDURE   **NOTE**   **SEE ALSO**   **KEYBOARD SHORTCUT**

When related material is in a different part, the part number will be included with the name of the section.

PART

INTRODUCING SYSTEM 7

When you turn on your Macintosh, you see the *Desktop*, shown in Figure I.1. It consists of a menu bar at the top of the screen, a work area, and assorted icons. *Icons* are graphic representations of files, applications, folders, disks, and other system elements.

USING THE MOUSE

You use the *mouse* to communicate with the Mac. When you move the mouse, an onscreen *pointer* moves correspondingly. Depending upon your application, the pointer can be an arrow,

an I-beam,

or a crosshair.

$+$

Following is a brief description of mouse movements.

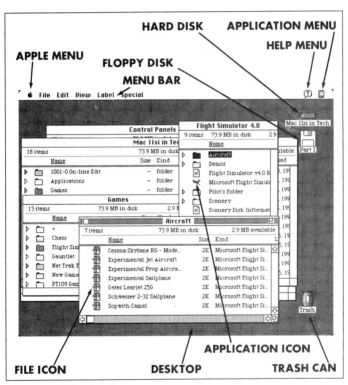

Figure 1.1: The Desktop

Pointing, Clicking, and Dragging

Pointing is positioning the mouse such that the pointer is on the item you want. Ideally, you should roll the mouse on a flat surface. Watch the pointer onscreen as you move the mouse, and you will see that the pointer moves the same distance and direction as the mouse.

 PROCEDURE

To select an icon or other object, click on it. The item appears highlighted. To click on an item, point to it and, without moving the mouse, rapidly press and release the mouse button.

 PROCEDURE

To open an icon, double-click on it. Again, you must first point to the object. Then quickly press and release the mouse button *twice.*

 PROCEDURE

To drag an item, point to it and hold down the mouse button. Move the mouse as you hold down the mouse button. Release the button when the item is where you want it to be.

SEE ALSO

Part IV, The Control Panels

A TOUR OF THE DESKTOP

The *Finder,* a system application, opens automatically every time you turn on the computer. You can use the Finder to organize documents, folders, and applications, to work with disks, and to access applications.

Although the Finder is always available, it is not always *active.* The active application is the one you're working in. For example, when you create text, your word processor is active. With System 7, though, MultiFinder is always available: You can open several applications at once and switch from one to the other, even copying text and graphics between different applications. Each time you open a new program, its name and icon are added to the *Application* menu. The icon of the active application displays at the far right of the menu bar. The number of programs you can open is limited only by the amount of memory on your Macintosh.

When you are working with an application, clicking anywhere on the open space of the Desktop activates the Finder. You can also activate the Finder by selecting it from the *Application* menu.

Dialog Boxes

When the Mac wants to communicate with you, it uses a *dialog box,* such as the one shown in Figure I.2. You tell the Mac what to do by clicking on one of the displayed *buttons* in the dialog box. To select the button that is heavily outlined, press Return. Sometimes you can type information into a dialog box. Or, you might see options displayed in a list with *checkboxes.* Clicking a checkbox selects its option and displays an *X* in the box. Clicking the box again deselects the option. Some dialog boxes list options with small round buttons. Clicking on the button selects the option.

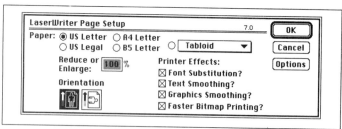

Figure I.2: A dialog box

When you are working in an application, you use a *directory dialog box*, illustrated in Figure I.3, to locate files. If the file you want is not on the disk currently displayed, click the Desktop button to display all available disks. You can then choose the correct disk.

If you do something questionable, an *alert box* might appear, accompanied by a sound. Figure I.4 shows the alert box that appears when you empty the trash. Alert boxes usually give you information and options.

Finder Windows

Information on the Desktop is displayed in *windows*. You can open a window, move it around the Desktop, change its size, scroll through it, and edit its contents.

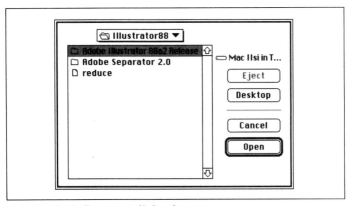

Figure I.3: A directory dialog box

A window that shows the contents of a disk or a folder is called a *Finder window.* Figure I.5 is an example of a Finder window. Folder and disk icons open into windows. You can have many windows open at one time—moving from window to window as you work with different files. To activate a window, bringing it to the front, just click on it. The title bar of an active window is lined.

A typical Finder window comprises the following elements:

▲ *Title bar*   A lined titled bar indicates that the window is active. Drag the title bar to reposition the window.

▲ *Window title*   The window's title is in the title bar. If you are buried deep in a hierarchy of windows, holding down ⌘ and clicking on a window's title displays a pop-up menu of its path. Hold down the mouse button and drag down the menu to select a folder or disk. Your selection will either open or become the active window.

Figure I.4: An alert box

▲ *Zoom box*   The zoom box is in the upper-right corner of the title bar. You resize an open window by clicking on the zoom box. The new, improved zoom box expands the window size just enough to display the list of files or file icons, but no more. Holding down the Option key and clicking the zoom box expands the window to its maximum size.

▲ *Close box*   The close box is in the upper-left corner of the window. Click on the close box to close a window.

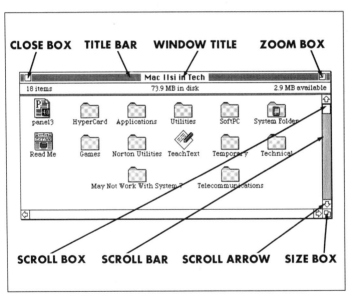

Figure 1.5: A Finder window

▲ *Size box*   The size box is in the lower-right corner of the title bar. Drag the size box to adjust the size of the window.

▲ *Scroll bars*   There are two scroll bars—vertical and horizontal. A grey bar indicates that there is additional content beyond the window's borders. A clear bar indicates that all contents of the directory are visible. Clicking in the scroll bar replaces the contents of the window with the next windowful of information.

▲ *Scroll box*   There are scroll boxes on each scroll bar. Dragging the scroll box displays a different part of the window's contents.

▲ *Scroll arrow*   Placing the pointer on one of the scroll arrows and holding down the mouse button shows you more of the contents of the window. Release the mouse button when the item you want scrolls into view.

 KEYBOARD SHORTCUTS

▲ ⌘-Option-down arrow opens the selected item and closes the current window.

▲ ⌘-W closes the active window.

▲ ⌘-Option-W closes all the Finder windows on the Desktop.

▲ ⌘-up arrow opens or makes active the parent-folder window.

▲ ⌘-Option-up arrow closes the current window, opening its parent-folder window.

▲ ⌘-down arrow opens or makes active the selected item.

Organizing Files

There are probably several different types of files visible on your Finder desktop—applications, data documents, system software files, utilities, fonts, dictionaries, and so on. One useful way of organizing such a hodge-podge of files is to group like files into *subfolders* and group subfolders together in *parent folders*. A parent folder is a folder that contains folders. For example, you might create parent folders on your hard disk for data files, applications, system files, utilities, and such. Then, within the application folder, you might have subfolders for PageMaker, Word, Excel, MacDraw II, etc., as shown in Figure I.6.

SEE ALSO

▲ *Part V, The File Menu*

▲ *Part V, The Application Menu*

11

Working with a Window's Contents

You can rename, copy, move, open, and discard files and folders from the Finder—without opening the Finder menus. Read *Part V, The Finder* for information on the keyboard shortcuts in the *Apple, File, Edit, View, Label, Special, Help,* and *Application* menus.

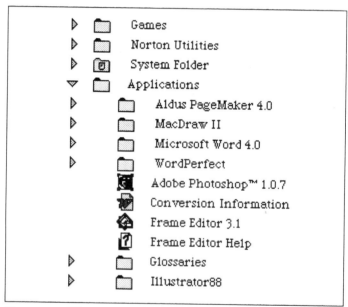

Figure 1.6: Files and folders in list view

PROCEDURE

To select a single file or folder, point to the item and click the mouse. You can click on either the icon itself or its name to select it. When you select an item, it appears highlighted.

Once highlighted, you can copy, open, move, or discard the item.

 KEYBOARD SHORTCUTS

▲ An arrow key selects the next icon in its direction.

▲ The tab key selects the next icon in alphabetical order by name.

▲ A letter key selects the first icon whose name begins with that letter.

 PROCEDURE

To select a contiguous group of icons, place the pointer at the top of the list and click the mouse button. While

holding down the button, drag down until all the icons
you want are selected. Selecting icons is similar; you drag
diagonally instead of downward. The Finder window will
scroll if the cursor hits one of its edges. The items that
are selected appear highlighted. You can then copy,
move, or discard the items.

 PROCEDURE

To select a non-contiguous group of icons, hold down
the Shift key. Then point to and click on each icon you
wish to select. The selected items will appear highlighted.

▷ ◼ `Capture Utilities`
    ▯ FINDER
▷ ▭ games
    ▯ MacDraw II Options
    ◼ `nbd resume`
    ◼ `newsletter`
▷ ▭ pictures
▷ ▭ Quicken
▷ ▭ randy
    ◼ `Standard Glossary`

You can then copy, move, or discard the items as a group.

KEYBOARD SHORTCUT

⌘-A selects all items in the active window.

NOTES

▲ Any part of a file name or icon inside the selection
rectangle will be selected. Previously, only those
files *completely* within the rectangle were selected.

▲ You can now select groups of files using this
method in all views. Previously, you could only do
this when viewing *by Icon* or *by Small Icon.*

PROCEDURE

To copy a file or folder from one window to another, drag the file or folder while holding down the Option key.

 PROCEDURE

To move a file or folder, drag the document or folder icon to the icon of the folder you want to put it in. In System 7, you can select *any* visible icon in any window and drag it to a new location without the source window becoming active. The icon appears at its new location when you release the mouse button.

 PROCEDURE

To move a window without making it active, drag it by the title bar while holding down the ⌘ key.

 PROCEDURE

To open a file or folder, double-click its icon. Or, highlight it and press ⌘-down arrow.

There may be times when you want to open a document with a program other than the one that created it. Drag the document's icon to a program icon and release the mouse button. If the program can open the document, it will do so. If not, nothing will happen.

 KEYBOARD SHORTCUT

⌘-O opens the selected icon.

 PROCEDURE

To rename a file or folder, follow these steps:

1. Click on the icon's name or select the icon and press Return. A box appears around the name

2. Type the new name.

3. Save by clicking outside the icon or pressing Return.

 PROCEDURE

To edit an icon's name, follow these steps:

1. Select the name by clicking it.

2. Point to the icon's name and click to place the I-beam where you want to edit the name.

3. You can insert text by typing it. You can replace text by dragging the I-beam over a portion of the name to highlight it and then typing.

4. Save by pressing Return or clicking outside the icon.

 PROCEDURE

To discard an icon from a Finder window, drag it to the Trash icon. The Trash will bulge.

Trash

The item will not be deleted, though, until you select *Empty Trash* from the *Special* menu.

 SEE ALSO

Part V, The Special Menu

WHAT'S NEW IN SYSTEM 7? ▲

With the advent of System 7, the Mac's power and versatility have been greatly expanded. In fact, it is so advanced, we will have to wait for software developers to write new applications before we can take full advantage of System 7's new features. Here are two significant examples:

▲ *Apple Events* System 7 has laid the groundwork for applications to communicate by developing an information interchange called AppleEvents. Apple-Events lets an application send messages to other applications. System 7 stores the messages and forwards them when the application is opened. It also dispatches messages across a network to applications on other Macs. When implemented, applications will be able to share features with each other—a word processor might ask a spellchecking application to look for errors, for example.

▲ *Data Access Manager (DAM)* Data Access Manager provides an easy way to get data from large network or mainframe databases. When DAM is supported, you can use a spreadsheet or word-processing application to get information from databases without knowing their specific query language.

Following are brief descriptions of System 7's new features—arranged in alphabetical order. More detailed information can be found in subsequent parts of this book.

Aliases

An alias is a small (only 1K to 3K) stand-in for the original item. You can make an alias of a file, folder, or disk and put it on the Desktop, in the *Apple* menu, or some other accessible place. Then programs, documents, and folders that you use frequently are right there when you need them!

SEE ALSO

Part V, The File Menu

Apple Menu

You can access documents, folders, applications, fonts, sounds, and control panels from the *Apple* menu. The *Apple* Menu can show up to fifty items.

SEE ALSO

▲ *Part II, Installing System 7*

▲ *Part III, The System Folder*

Comments

Comments are entered in the Get Info window. You can display comments in a list of files and search for files by comment text.

SEE ALSO

Part V, The File Menu

Control Panels

Control panel documents are stored in a special Control Panels folder within the System Folder. An alias of the folder displays in the *Apple* menu.

SEE ALSO

Part IV, The Control Panels

Customizing Icons

You can customize how icons appear in Finder windows, with much more control over the way items display. You can

▲ Design your own icons and replace the icons of most files, folders, disks, or applications.

▲ Set the font and size of icon names.

▲ Set the way items align in icon view.

SEE ALSO

▲ *Part IV, The Control Panels*

▲ *Part V, The File Menu*

Desk Accessories

Now desk accessories work just like any other application. They can be stored in the *Apple* menu, on the Desktop, or in any other place you want. Best of all, you no longer need the Font/DA Mover program to install them.

SEE ALSO

▲ *Part II, Installing System 7*

▲ *Part III, The System Folder*

Editing Icon Names

Clicking an icon no longer selects the name for editing. Previously, you could select the icon and type a new name, meaning you could accidentally hit the keyboard while the icon was selected and rename it unintentionally. You must actually select the name now.

 SEE ALSO

Working with Window's Contents

Multitasking

Under System 7, MultiFinder is always available. You can open as many applications as your memory will allow, then switch among applications, return to the Finder to launch new programs, find documents, and perform file management tasks. System 7 lists open applications under the *Application* menu rather than under the *Apple* menu.

 SEE ALSO

Part V, The Application Menu

File Sharing

If your Mac is connected to a network, System 7 lets you share hard drives, folders, and files with other network users.

SEE ALSO

▲ *Part II, Installing System 7*

▲ *Part VI, Sharing Files and Programs*

Find Command

The new Find command offers expanded search capabilities. It will actually open the folder that contains the item you are searching for, and you can specify multiple search parameters.

SEE ALSO

Part V, The File Menu

Finder

There are two new permanent menus at the right end of the title bar: the *Help* menu and the *Application* menu. Read *Part V* for a description of the commands you can choose from these menus. The following describes some of the new Finder improvements:

   ▲ *Navigation* Under System 7, you can scroll windows automatically. You can drag an item past the active area of the window. You can also drag diagonally into a window corner. Dragging an item from one window to another now lets you keep the destination window in view.

▲ *Zooming* You can zoom a window just enough to show all items in it by clicking the zoom box.

▲ *Selecting items* You can select multiple items by dragging over them in list view. You can even select items from different levels.

▲ *Opening documents* You can open any document from the Finder by dragging its icon to the icon of an application that is capable of opening it.

▲ *New directory dialog box* A list of all available disks can be displayed by clicking on the Desktop button in the Open and Save dialog boxes.

▲ *Pop-up Menus* You can also go to the Desktop by choosing it from the pop-up menu in the title bar. If you hold ⌘ and click on a window's title, a pop-up menu will appear, showing the directory path of the open folder. You can choose a folder or disk from the listing.

Help

Point to any object and information about the object will appear in a balloon. You can turn balloon help on or off from the *Help* menu.

SEE ALSO

Part II, The Application Menu

Hiding Windows

You can avoid the clutter of multiple open windows by selecting the *Hide* command from the *Application* menu. A hidden application is still open. If the application is performing a background operation when you hide it, the operation continues.

SEE ALSO

Part II, The Application Menu

Keyboard Control

Without using the mouse, you can select an item, open an item, move through, open, and close folders.

Labels

You can assign a label to each icon and view the contents of a window by label. The label displays only in a list view. If your computer has a color or grayscale monitor, you can also assign a color.

SEE ALSO

▲ *Part IV, The Control Panels*

▲ *Part V, The Label Menu*

Memory Management

While you are working, the Mac keeps applications and other current information in *random-access memory* (RAM). Since RAM is limited and many applications use a lot of it, accessing increased RAM is a high priority. System 7's Memory control panel lets you manage and extend your computer's memory. Following is a brief description of System 7's memory features. If your Macintosh model cannot make use of 32-Bit Addressing and Virtual Memory, they will not appear as options.

▲ A *disk cache* is a portion of RAM that the Mac allocates for applications to store information. You can adjust the disk cache using the Memory control panel.

▲ *32-Bit Addressing* is a new method of addressing memory chips that lets you install and use more RAM.

▲ *Virtual Memory* lets you increase the amount of available memory without installing more RAM. With Virtual Memory turned on, System 7 sets aside a certain amount of space on your hard disk and uses it as if it were RAM.

SEE ALSO

Part IV, The Control Panels

Window Views

Windows can display their contents in several list views. Items display in an outline format letting you see, copy, and move items from nested folders in the same window. You can expand or compress the outline to show or hide the contents of a folder. You can:

▲ Determine the information that displays in list views.

▲ Choose whether to show folder sizes and disk information in all views.

▲ Search for files without opening multiple windows, which makes copying and moving files much easier.

▲ Change the order of items in list view by clicking on the column heading.

SEE ALSO

Part IV, The Control Panels

Publish and Subscribe

If an application has this feature, you can link information so that any changes to original information in a file, the *publisher,* automatically update in *subscribers* of it. Updates can occur within your system or across a network.

SEE ALSO

Part V, The File Menu

Stationery Pads

Stationery pads are templates. Create a document with the elements you want to reuse in subsequent documents. Then, convert the document to a stationery pad. Each time you open the stationery pad you get a new document with all the elements preset.

SEE ALSO

Part V, The File Menu

System Folder

The System Folder has been reorganized. System files are put into special folders rather than left floating loose.

SEE ALSO

▲ *Part II, Installing System 7*

▲ *Part III, The System Folder*

Trash Can

You must empty the Trash manually using the *Empty Trash* command on the *Special* menu. An alert dialog box informs you of how many items are in the Trash and how much disk space they occupy, asking whether you want to permanently discard the items. You can disable the alert, but there is no longer a way to automatically discard items.

SEE ALSO

▲ *Part V, The Special Menu*

▲ *Part V, The File Menu*

TrueType Fonts

TrueType fonts are *scalable* outline fonts that will print and display sharp text regardless of size. You can install fonts by dragging them to the system file, eliminating the Font/DA Mover utility. Double-click on a font icon to display a font sample.

SEE ALSO

▲ *Part II, Installing System 7*

▲ *Part III, The System Folder*

PART

INSTALLING

SYSTEM 7

To install System 7 on a Macintosh computer, you need a hard-disk drive, at least 2 Mb (megabytes) of random-access memory (RAM), and a floppy-disk drive. You should probably have about 5 Mb of free hard-disk space as well. If you are a new Mac user, you can disregard a lot of the following information. Just make sure any new software you add is compatible with System 7 and use the Easy Install method.

To take full advantage of System 7, it must be properly installed. Therefore, it is important you do the following:

▲ *Back up all data on your hard drive.*

▲ Make copies of the System 7 installation disks.

▲ Use a disk utility to check your hard disk(s). Disks can be damaged by heavy use. Make sure yours is in good shape. Then, if you have problems after installation, you'll know the problem lies elsewhere.

▲ Evaluate your existing software to determine whether or not it is compatible with System 7.

▲ Search for other System Files and remove all but one.

We will examine each of the steps in depth.

CHECKING YOUR HARD DISK

If you have an Apple hard disk, checking it with Disk First Aid is sufficient. However, if you have a hard disk manufactured by another company, it is a good idea to call them and ask whether their disk is compatible with System 7. They might have special utilities for their brand.

 PROCEDURE

To check your hard disk for damage, follow these steps:

1. Restart the Mac, using "Disk Tools" as the startup disk. It is one of your System 7 disks. The Disk Tools icon displays above your hard-disk icon.

2. Double-click to open Disk Tools and then double-click the Disk First Aid icon.

3. Select the hard drive you want to check and click Open.

4. Click Start. If Disk First Aid indicates that minor repairs are needed, click OK. If you get a message

saying the disk is damaged and cannot be repaired, use the HD SC Setup program to test the disk further.

5. Double-click the HD SC Setup icon, and select your hard disk. Click Test. Depending upon the test results, you might be able to repair the problem by using a disk-repair utility or, if all else fails, reinitializing the disk. Proceed with caution. Make copies of all your files, because reinitializing *completely erases a disk.*

6. Choose *Quit* from the *File* menu.

EVALUATING YOUR SOFTWARE ▲

Apple provides a HyperCard stack called the *Compatibility Checker* to help you determine the compatibility of your software with System 7. To use the Compatibility Checker, it must be in the same folder as HyperCard 1.2.2 or later and the Home stack.

 PROCEDURE

To run the Compatibility Checker, follow these steps:

1. Insert the disk "Before You Install System 7" into your floppy-disk drive.

2. Double-click to open the disk icon and copy the Compatibility Checker to your hard disk. It will not run from a floppy.

3. Double-click the Compatibility Checker icon. The Welcome screens display, followed by the Introduction screen shown in Figure II.1.

4. Click the Start Checking button and the Compatibility Checker will examine the files on your hard disk. Relax—it takes a while. When it finishes, the Compatibility Checker will offer to move any questionable or incompatible items from the Sytem Folder to a new folder named *May*

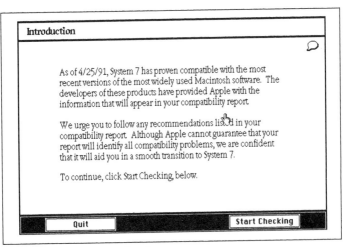

Figure showing the Introduction screen with the following text:

Introduction

As of 4/25/91, System 7 has proven compatible with the most recent versions of the most widely used Macintosh software. The developers of these products have provided Apple with the information that will appear in your compatibility report.

We urge you to follow any recommendations listed in your compatibility report. Although Apple cannot guarantee that your report will identify all compatibility problems, we are confident that it will aid you in a smooth transition to System 7.

To continue, click Start Checking, below.

Quit   Start Checking

Figure II.1: The Introduction screen

Not Work With System 7. See Figure II.2. A dialog box verifies the move. Click OK.

5. When all files have been examined, a report displays listing suspect items and their status. Read the report carefully. It explains the compatibility-status codes, provides specific information about your software, and gives names and telephone numbers of software developers. An example of the report is shown in Figure II.3. It is a good idea to call the software developer when you are unsure of a product's compatibility status. But beware! Although not always obvious, incompatibilities can cause serious problems over time.

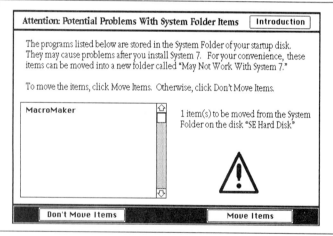

Figure II.2: Moving incompatible items

6. You can save the report by clicking the Save
Report button. It's a good idea to save the report
(or print it out), as you will want to refer to it later.
You can print the report by clicking the Print
Report button.

7. Click the Quit button.

8. If you have moved items to the May Not Work
With System 7 folder, you will be prompted to
restart the computer before installing System 7.
(The items will remain active until you restart.)
Click OK if you see this prompt, as shown in
Figure II.4.

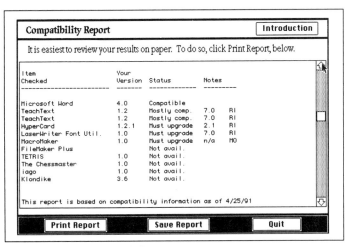

Figure II.3: A compatibility report

REMOVING OLD SYSTEM FILES ▲

Your System Folder might include only files included by Apple with your particular version of the system software. However, if you have purchased applications, fonts, or desk accessories (programs you can launch from the *Apple* menu), you have added files to the System Folder. A system file can be any of the following:

▲ *Inits*—small startup programs that add features to the Finder or the system software. These small programs are referred to in System 7 as *system extensions*.

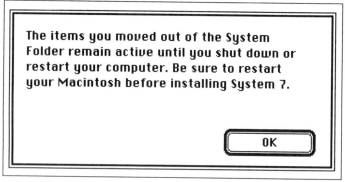

Figure II.4: The restart dialog box

▲ *Cdevs* or *control panel devices*—these are stored in the Control Panels folder. Under System 7, a control panel is a small, independent application that can be launched just like any other application. These programs let you customize various Macintosh features, such as startup disk, sound, color, memory, and so on.

▲ *Printer* or *network drivers*—software that allows the Mac to use certain printers or devices.

▲ *Preference files*, *help files*, and *dictionaries*—application-related programs.

These files should go into the System Folder itself. At this time, some preference files will not operate properly if placed in the Preferences folder. Opening the System Folder lets you place files where you want. If you drag the files onto the System Folder icon, the Mac places them for you.

You cannot rely on the Apple Compatibility Checker for a definitive answer to whether your existing system files will work under System 7. Also, updating your current System Folder has a risk: It's not uncommon for the System, Finder, and other non-system files to sustain minor but undetectable damage through ordinary use. The damage can affect the update, potentially causing serious problems in the future. The cautious approach is to move *all* System files from your current System Folder to a new folder.

INSTALLING SYSTEM 7

Then, delete the current System Folder and install System 7. After installing System 7, you can manually reinstall any of your old resources.

 PROCEDURE

To remove system files, follow these steps:

1. Restart the Mac with the "Apple Utilities" disk containing the System Folder. You must use a floppy disk to start up because you cannot remove an active system file.

2. Create a new folder and name it *Later.*

3. Open both Later and your old System Folder and arrange the desktop so you can view the contents of both. You are going to copy the system files to the Later folder.

4. Use the Font/DA Mover to copy the installed fonts into a new suitcase file in the Later folder.

5. Copy the printer fonts to the Later folder.

6. Use the Font/DA Mover to copy the installed desk accessories into new suitcase files in the Later folder.

7. Copy any sounds you have installed, using the utility with which you originally installed them.

8. Copy the rest of your system resource files into the Later folder. You might want to sort these files into folders within the Later folder.

9. Copy the May Not Work With System 7 folder into the Later folder.

10. Drag the System Folder to the trash and empty the trash. If you can't remove the System Folder, check the contents for locked files. If you find a locked file, highlight it, select *Get Info* from the *File* menu, and click on the Locked box to clear it. Then, try again!

INSTALLING SYSTEM 7

Unlike previous Macintosh system software, System 7 *requires* you to use the Installer program. Deactivate any virus-detection software or it will interfere with the installation. (Before doing so, you might wish to scan each of the new system disks.)

You can install from a floppy-disk drive, a hard disk, a file server, or a System 7 CD-ROM. To install from a file server or a CD-ROM drive, first copy the System 7 installation files onto your hard drive. (Copy each installation disk into its own folder). Make sure you have copied the installation files onto your startup drive. If you are installing from a file server, use the Chooser to mount the volume containing the installation folder.

Do *not* install the 32-bit addressing option on a Macintosh Plus, Classic, II, II LC, IIx, IIcx, SE/30 or

Portable. Do *not* install virtual memory on the Plus,
Classic, II, II LC, or portable.

You can install in two ways: Easy Install or custom
installation.

Easy Install

Easy Install is an automated process for installing the
System 7 software. You have little control over options,
though. Use this method if you are a new Mac user or if
your current system is fairly basic and you are sure your
installed system resources are compatible with System 7.

 PROCEDURE

To use the Easy Install method, follow these steps:

1. Choose *Shut Down* from the *Special* menu.

2. Restart the Mac using your copy of the "Install 1"
   disk. If you're installing from a file server or CD-
   ROM disk, open the Installer program inside the
   Install I folder. An information screen displays.

3. Click the OK button. You'll see a screen like the
   one shown in Figure II.5.

4. Click the Switch Disk button if the displayed
   hard-disk name is not the one on which you
   want to install System 7.

5. Click the Install button. If you get a message during the Easy Install telling you there is insufficient space to complete the installation, you can install just the minimal software using the custom method, discussed next.

6. If you're installing from a floppy-disk drive, insert the appropriate disks as Installer prompts you.

7. If the installation is successful, you will see a message to this effect, and you can safely click Quit. If the installation fails, see the section on installation problems at the end of this part.

8. Restart the Mac, and you will be running under System 7.

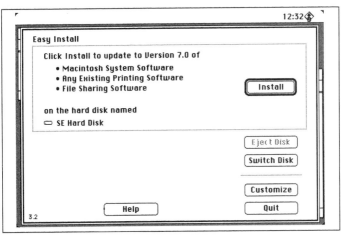

Figure II.5: The Install screen

Custom Installation

Custom installation gives you a great deal of flexibility in your software configuration. With this method, you can select specific system resources you want installed. For example, you might want to save disk space by not installing printer and network drivers until you need them. You can install resources at any time.

Here are some guidelines for selecting resources:

▲ If you want to run your Macintosh on a *network,* select *System Software for any Macintosh* and *Software for all Apple Printers.*

▲ Select a *printer driver* for every installed printer.

▲ If you want to *share* folders and volumes with other Macintoshes, select *File Sharing Software.* If your Macintosh will be part of an Ethertalk or Tokentalk network, select the appropriate network driver.

▲ Select only one *System Software* option. Make sure it is the one for your particular Macintosh model.

▲ Select the *Minimal System Software* option if you have limited free space on your hard drive. You can also use this option to put System 7 on a 1.44 Mb floppy disk.

PROCEDURE

To install using the custom method, follow these steps:

1. Choose *Shut Down* from the *Special* menu.

2. Restart the Mac using your copy of the "Install 1" disk. If you're installing from a file server or CD-ROM disk, open the Installer program inside the Install I folder. An information screen displays.

3. Click the OK button. You'll see a screen like the one shown in Figure II.5.

4. Click the Switch Disk button if the displayed harddisk name is not the one on which you want to install System 7.

5. Click the Customize button. A list of resources will appear. Study the guidelines for selecting resources, described in the preceding section, *Custom Installation.* Click on each resource you want to install, as illustrated in Figure II.6. If you want to select multiple resources, hold down the Shift key as you click on each option.

6. Double-check your selections. When you are satisfied, click Install.

INSTALLING SYSTEM 7

7. If you're installing from a floppy-disk drive, insert the appropriate disks as Installer prompts you.

8. If the installation is successful, you can either Quit or Continue. Clicking Quit lets you either turn off or restart your Mac. Clicking Continue returns you to the Install screen, where you can perform other installations. If the installation fails, see the section on installation problems at the end of this part.

9. Restart the Mac, and you will be running under System 7.

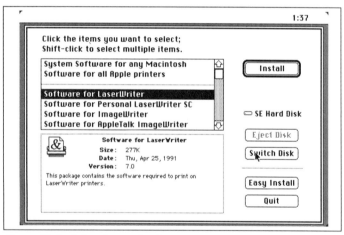

Figure II.6: Selecting a single resource

REINSTALLING OLD SYSTEM FILES ▲

If you have used the custom installation method, you will need to reinstall the old system files you saved to the Later folder. If you used Easy Install, the Installer took care of this task for you.

 PROCEDURE

To reinstall system files, follow these steps:

1. Open both your start-up disk and the Later folder. Arrange your desktop so you can view both the System and Later folders. You are going to copy software files from Later to the new System Folder.

2. To install screen fonts, double-click on each suitcase file in the Later folder. Highlight all the fonts and drag them onto the System Folder *icon.* The Installer will examine the files and place them in the appropriate folder. A dialog box tells you where they will be copied. Click the OK button. Installer will automate this process if you drag the files into an *open* System Folder.

3. To install desk accessories (DAs), double-click on each suitcase file to open it. Then highlight each desk accessory and drag them onto the

System Folder *icon*. The Installer again examines
the files and places them in the appropriate
folder. Figure II.7 shows the dialog box that tells
you where the files will be copied. Click the OK
button. Desk Accessories are small application
programs. Previously, they were only accessible
from the Apple menu. Their usefulness was their
constant availability. In System 7, with Multi-
Finder always on, these DA's can be launched
just like any other application.

4. To install system extension documents (*inits*) and
control panels devices (*cdevs*) in the System Folder,
drag each file onto the System Folder icon. The Installer will examine the files and place them in the
appropriate folder, as before. A dialog box tells
you where the files will be copied. Click the OK
button.

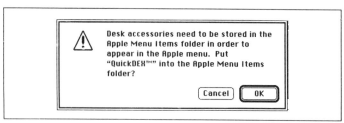

Figure II.7: Installing desk accessories

5. Open your System Folder to finish installing the rest of your old system files (help, preferences, dictionaries, and so on). Select the files and drag them into the open System Folder.

6. Select printer font files and drag them into the open System Folder.

7. Click OK to respond to the dialog box.

8. Restart the Macintosh. You are ready to explore System 7 and its functions.

 NOTE

Install questionable inits and cdevs in the System Folder one by one, restarting the Mac after each installation. If the Mac crashes on startup, see the appropriate section under *Troubleshooting*.

TROUBLESHOOTING

If the installation fails, a dialog box will display, telling you what the problem is. Usually, an Installer file is either missing or damaged or there is a problem with the hard disk.

Missing or Damaged Installer Files

If you get a message indicating one of your Installer files is either missing or damaged, make a new copy of the installation disks and reinstall. If the installation fails again, get a new set of Installer files.

Hard Disk Problems

If you get a message indicating there is a problem with your hard disk, update the hard-disk driver using the setup software that came with the hard drive. Be careful not to reinitialize or reformat the hard disk, which erases everything on it. Then try installing again. But don't take chances: back up your data!

If that doesn't work, back up your hard drive and reformat it. If you do not have the original formatting software, use a commercial package.

The Mac Crashes on Startup

The problem could be an incompatible init or cdev. Restart the Mac while holding down the Shift key.

This disables system extensions, allowing the Mac to start up. If you have been installing the startup documents one at a time, open the System Folder and remove the problem file.

If you installed them all at once, remove them all and reinstall them one by one, as described in the section *Reinstalling Old System Files.*

PART

THE SYSTEM

FOLDER

The *System Folder* is the heart of the Macintosh. It contains the System file, system extensions, and various application-related files. You will encounter the following files and folders:

▲ The *System file,* used by the Macintosh to start up and operate the computer. It stores the system's fonts, sounds, and keyboard files.

▲ *Applications* that expand the functionality of the system software. Examples are system extensions (inits), control-panel devices (cdevs), and printer or network drivers. Apple includes some of these small programs with each System, but you may wish to add others—many good commercial applications are available.

▲ *Application files* stored in the System Folder or one of the subfolders for reasons of efficiency and security. These do not necessarily work directly with the system software. These files include printer fonts, Word's *Temp* files, PageMaker 4.0's Aldus folder, and so on.

WHAT'S NEW?

The System 7 System Folder has been completely redesigned. Previous System Folders were cluttered affairs. It used to be just as hard to find what you needed in the System Folder as it is to find a missing sock in a dresser drawer filled with a jumble of clothes.

The new System Folder's organization, though, far surpasses that of its predecessor. Based on a series of *subfolders*—Apple Menu Items, Control Panels, Extensions, Preferences, PrintMonitor Documents, and Startup Items—you can always find what you want quickly and easily, as shown in Figure III.1. Each subfolder is designed to store specific types of files. Because it is very important that System Folder files be placed in their appropriate subfolder, the installation has been largely automated.

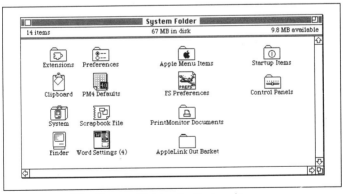

Figure III.1: The System Folder in System 7

THE SYSTEM FOLDER

If you do have files that you're not sure what to do with, the Easy Install program can place them for you.

This part also gives you information on the type of files appropriate for each of these subfolders and on the System file itself. The only subfolder we will not examine is the Control Panels Folder, which is discussed in detail in *Part IV.*

EXPLORING THE
SYSTEM FILE ▲

A selection of *fonts* and *sounds* are placed in the System file during installation. In addition to these you can install any third-party fonts or sounds you wish. Installing fonts is simple, because Apple has done away with the Font/DA Mover.

TrueType vs.
PostScript Fonts

TrueType is a new font format developed by Apple. TrueType fonts are *scalable*, which means the font can be scaled to any size. A single TrueType font file contains mathematical descriptions of *both* screen and print characters. So TrueType fonts can display clearly onscreen (without jagged edges) and then print at high resolution on a dot-matrix, Quick Draw, or PostScript printer.

Conversely, *PostScript* fonts consist of two files: a screen-font file and a printer-font file. PostScript screen fonts are *bitmap* or fixed-size fonts. PostScript printer fonts contain mathematical descriptions of each character. The printer uses these descriptions to produce high-quality output. For each screen font used in a document, the corresponding printer font must be available at print time. Otherwise, the printer substitutes a bitmap font and your output looks dreadful.

TrueType fonts are designed to work with other font formats, rather than replace them. If a particular font, such as Times, is available in both fixed-size and TrueType, the Macintosh will use the fixed-size font. TrueType is used only when you select a font size that is unavailable in the fixed-size format.

If you wish to use a TrueType font for standard point sizes such as 10, 12, 14, 18, and 24, you must remove the corresponding fixed-sized font from the System file. If you do this, however, old documents created with fixed-size formats will reformat when printed with the True-Type format. You must decide which is preferable.

You can differentiate TrueType fonts from fixed-size screen fonts by their respective icons: The TrueType icon displays three symbols whereas the fixed-size font icon displays only one.

PROCEDURE

To view a font, follow these steps:

1. Double-click on the System file icon to open it.

2. Click on a TrueType-font icon. Three sizes of type-style display, as shown in Figure III.2.

3. Click on a fixed-size font icon. One type size displays, as shown in Figure III.3.

 PROCEDURE

To install fonts, follow these steps:

1. Quit any open applications.

2. Drag the font file or suitcase you wish to install on top of the System Folder icon (you don't need to open the System Folder).

3. A dialog box will confirm the operation.

 PROCEDURE

To install selected fonts from a suitcase, follow these steps:

1. Quit any open applications.

2. Double-click to open the suitcase file.

3. Hold down Shift and click once on the font names you want to install.

4. Open the System Folder icon.

5. Drag the selected fonts onto the System file.

6. Close the suitcase file and the System Folder.

Figure III.2: TrueType Times (bold, italic)

PROCEDURE

To remove fonts, follow these steps:

1. Quit any open application.

2. Double-click to open the System Folder.

3. Double-click on the System file to open it.

4. Drag the icons of any fonts you want to remove from both the System file and System Folder.

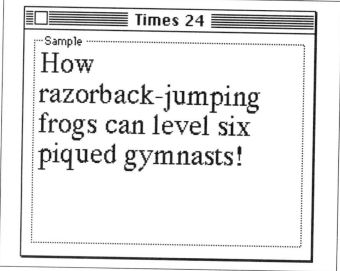

Figure III.3: Fixed-size Times 24

(You might want to create a special folder on your disk to store fonts you don't use regularly.)

 NOTE

PostScript printer fonts should be placed loose in the System Folder.

 SEE ALSO

Part V, The Font Menu

The World of Sound

The Macintosh interface is not merely visual; it is also aural. You can install sound files as easily as font files, playing them whenever you like and even changing the sound the Mac uses to get your attention.

 PROCEDURE

To play a sound, follow these steps:

1. Double-click on the System file icon to open it. Figure III.4 shows the contents of a typical System file.

2. Double-click on the sound icon. The sound plays.

 **SEE ALSO**

Part IV, Sound

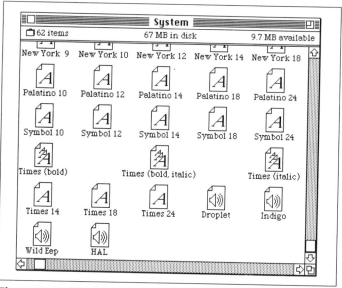

Figure III.4: The contents of the System file

PROCEDURE

To install sounds, follow these steps:

1. Quit any open applications.

2. Drag the sound file or suitcase you wish to install on top of the System Folder icon (you don't need to open the System Folder).

3. A dialog box will confirm the operation.

 PROCEDURE

To remove sounds, follow these steps:

1. Quit any open program.

2. Double-click to open the System Folder.

3. Double-click on the System file to open it.

4. Drag the icons of any sounds you want to remove from both the System file and System Folder.

 SEE ALSO

Part IV, Sound

THE APPLE MENU ITEMS FOLDER ▲

Storing programs, documents, folders, or aliases in the Apple Menu Items folder makes them accessible from the *Apple* menu (under the Apple icon on the far left of the menu bar). There is no longer a limit to the number of items you can put under the *Apple* menu, but only the first fifty will display.

Desk accessories are small, specialized applications. System 7 includes seven desk accessories—Alarm Clock, Calculator, Chooser, Key Caps, Note Pad, Puzzle, and Scrapbook. They are automatically placed in the Apple Menu Items folder during installation, as illustrated in Figure III.5. If you have a Macintosh Portable, Battery will be included as well. Although the Control Panels

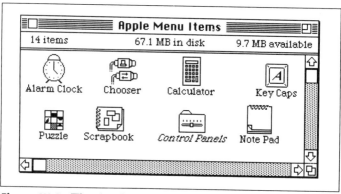

Figure III.5: The Apple Menu Items folder

folder is not a desk accessory, its *alias* is placed in the Apple Menu Items folder to make it easily accessible. (We will discuss aliases shortly.)

The Alarm Clock

The Alarm Clock desk accessory lets you set an alarm to remind you of appointments, meetings, and other engagements.

 PROCEDURE

To set the Alarm Clock, follow these steps:

1. Select the Alarm Clock from the *Apple* menu.

2. Click the small lever to the right of the time display. The lever will swing down, showing you the options illustrated in Figure III.6.

Figure III.6: The Alarm Clock options

3. Click the alarm-clock icon to select it. It will get excited, as shown in the figure.

4. Click on the hour, minutes, or seconds of the alarm time (just below the current time) to change them. Then click the up or down arrow or type the number you want.

5. Clicking the small button to the left of the alarm time turns the alarm on and off. If the button is up, the alarm is on.

6. Click the square button at the top left to close the Alarm Clock.

7. The alarm will sound at the time you have set. If the speaker volume is set to zero, the menu bar will flash once and an alarm-clock icon will flash on the left of the menu bar.

 NOTES

▲ Open the Alarm Clock and click on the small button to the left of the alarm time to turn off the alarm.

▲ You can set the Mac's internal date and time by clicking on the calendar and clock icons.

The Calculator

The calculator is a handy desk accessory that works as a four-function, pocket calculator. See Figure III.7. If you're working in an application, for example Quicken, and need to multiply some large numbers, this desk accessory can do the job. Results can be copied and pasted into application files.

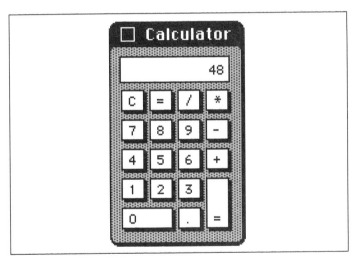

Figure III.7: The Calculator

The Chooser

The chooser is a desk accessory that lets you select a printer, output device, or network connection. See Figure III.8. If you are attached to a network, you can select the available disks and printers.

PROCEDURE

To select a printer, output device, or network connection, follow these steps:

1. Select the Chooser from the *Apple* menu.

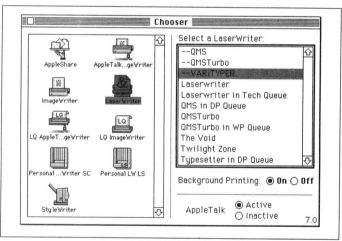

Figure III.8: The Chooser

2. Click the icon of the device you want to use.

3. If your network is divided into zones, you'll see a list of zones in the lower-left side of the Chooser. Click the name of the zone in which the device is located. A list of devices displays in the right-hand window of the Chooser. Select a device by clicking its name.

4. Close the Chooser. You can then use the selected device.

 KEYBOARD SHORTCUTS

▲ Press Tab to move from window to window in the Chooser area.

▲ Type a character to highlight a device name that begins with that character.

Key Caps

The Key Caps desk accessory, shown in Figure III.9, shows the location of characters for each font installed in the System file. By pressing one or more of the *modifier keys* (Option, Shift, and ⌘) in combination with certain character or number keys, you can produce a variety of optional characters.

PROCEDURE

To use Key Caps, follow these steps:

1. Select Key Caps from the *Apple* menu.

2. Select a font name from the *Key Caps* menu.

3. Press any of the modifier keys, or Option and Shift in combination, to see the location of optional characters.

4. Close Key Caps by clicking on the close box in the upper-left corner.

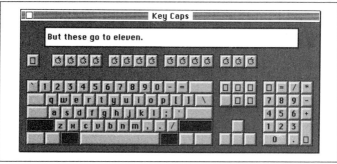

Figure III.9: Key Caps

PROCEDURE

To type accented characters, use the following key combinations:

To produce this	Type this
à	Option-`, then **a**
é	Option-e, then **e**
î	Option-i, then **i**
ñ	Option-n, then **n**
ü	Option-u, then **u**
ç	Option-c

The Note Pad

This desk accessory (See Figure III.10) is a handy place to store small amounts of information. It's easy to access, making it useful for jotting down notes or reminders while you're working on something else.

The Puzzle

No one can accuse the Mac of being stodgy. The Puzzle is a constant lure from work! See Figure III.11.

The Scrapbook

Text, graphics, and sounds can be saved in a Scrapbook file. Figure III.12 shows a graphic image in the Scrapbook.

Figure III.10: The Note Pad

Figure III.11: The Puzzle

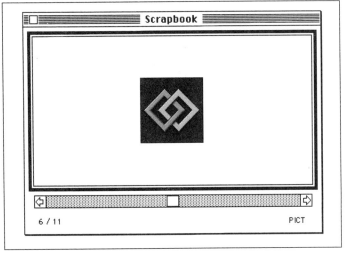

Figure III.12: The Scrapbook

As each Scrapbook file can hold only a limited number of items, you might want to create new Scrapbook files, save the old ones, and use them as needed.

 PROCEDURE

To use multiple Scrapbook files, follow these steps:

1. Rename the current Scrapbook file.

2. Drag the current Scrapbook file out of the System Folder.

3. Name the new file **Scrapbook File**.

4. Put the new Scrapbook file in the Apple Menu Items folder.

 **SEE ALSO**

Part V, The Finder

Adding Other Desk Accessories

Desk accessories are stored in suitcase files like the one shown in Figure III.13. A suitcase file can hold several desk accessories. Some are supplied by Apple and you can get others from third-party software developers.

PROCEDURE

To add desk accessories, follow these steps:

1. Double-click to open the suitcase file. Figure III.14 shows desk-accessory files stored in a suitcase.

2. Open the System Folder.

Figure III.13: A suitcase file icon

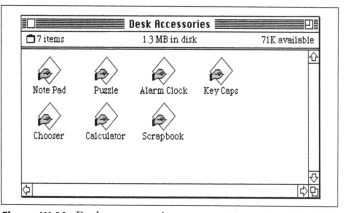

Figure III.14: Desk accessory icons

77

3. Drag the items you want from the suitcase file and put them in the Apple Menu Items folder. You can drag the empty suitcase to the Trash. The desk accessory will be available immediately under the *Apple* menu.

 PROCEDURE

To remove desk accessories, drag the desk accessory icons out of the Apple Menu Items folder. The name will disappear from under the *Apple* menu immediately.

Adding Applications, Documents, and Folders

If there are applications, documents, or folders you want to access easily, put them in the Apple Menu Items folder. Then, you can select them direclty from the *Apple* menu without having to hunt through folders. Alternately, you can place *aliases* in the Apple Menu Items folder, as discussed in the next section.

PROCEDURE

To add applications, documents, and folders, follow these steps:

1. Double-click to open your System Folder.

2. Select the application, document, or folder you wish to move.

3. Drag the item's icon to the Apple Menu Items folder. The item will be available immediately under the *Apple* menu.

 PROCEDURE

To remove applications, documents, and folders, drag the item's icon *out of* the Apple Menu Items folder. The name will disappear from under the *Apple* menu.

Adding Aliases

An *alias* is a representation of an original file. It is essentially a linked reference to the original application or file. The advantage of aliases is that you can make as many as you like for a given file. They are distinguished by italics. If you want to have quick access to a program, document, or shared disk that is buried in several layers of folders, you can make an alias for it and put the alias in the *Apple* menu. Then, any time you want to access the item, you can choose the item's alias from the *Apple* menu.

 PROCEDURE

To add aliases, follow these steps:

1. Double-click to open your System Folder.

2. Drag the alias' icon to the Apple Menu Items folder. It will display immediately under the *Apple* menu.

 PROCEDURE

To remove aliases, drag the item's icon out of the Apple Menu Items folder. The alias name disappears from under the *Apple* menu.

 **SEE ALSO**

Part V, The File Menu

THE EXTENSIONS FOLDER ▲

The Extensions folder is designed to store applications that affect the functionality of system software, either by expanding or modifying the system's capabilities. Examples include printer, scanner, and network *drivers,* as well as system extensions (*inits*). Figure III.15 shows the contents of a typical Extension folder. Yours may differ.

A *driver* is a program that allows the Mac to work with an external device. Whereas drivers become usuable upon installation, init files do not become active until

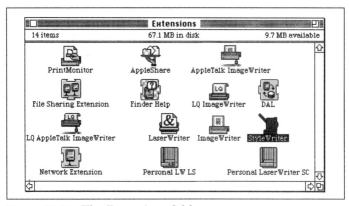

Figure III.15: The Extensions folder

THE SYSTEM FOLDER

you restart your computer. The PrintMonitor file is automatically placed in this folder during installation along
with printer drivers for each printer you intend to use.

At start-up, the system software checks the Extensions
folder. If you have trouble starting, the problem may be
an incompatible extension file. Disable and remove them
all from the Extensions folder. Then reinstall them one
by one.

 PROCEDURE

To disable extensions, follow these steps:

1. Hold down Shift while restarting the computer.
   This disables all extensions.

2. Remove them all and reinstall them one at a time.

3. Drag the incompatible file out of the System
   Folder.

 NOTE

Although inits are commonly referred to as *start-up
documents,* they are system extensions and belong in
the Extensions folder.

Determining File Types

It is not always clear whether a program is an *init* or a *cdev* (control panel device). As it is important to place items in the correct folder, Apple offers some help in determining an item's file-type classification.

PROCEDURE

To check a file's type, follow these steps:

1. Select the item.

2. Select *Get Info* from the *File* menu (⌘-I). The Kind category indicates the type of file you have selected, as displayed in Figure III.16.

NOTE

Some of your old init files may not operate properly in the Extensions folder. The difficulty might be that they can't function in a subfolder like the Extensions folder. In this case, try placing the init file at the top of level of the System Folder.

THE SYSTEM FOLDER

THE PREFERENCES FOLDER

The Preferences folder is designed to store application-related files. These files contain special settings that

---

```
▤☐▤▤▤      LaserWriter Info      ▤▤▤
```

LaserWriter
System Software v7.0

Kind: Chooser extension
Size: 219K on disk (223,926 bytes used)

Where: Mac IIsi in Tech : System Folder :
Extensions :

Created: Thu, Apr 25, 1991, 12:00 PM
Modified: Mon, Nov 4, 1991, 10:07 AM
Version: 7.0, © Apple Computer, Inc.
1983–1991

Comments:

☐ **Locked**

Figure III.16: The *Get Info* window

help the Mac work with an application. Preference files are usually created by applications and utilities. Aldus PageMaker, Microsoft Word, and Microsoft Excel, for example, create and maintain their own preference files.

When you install an application, any preference files generated will be placed in the folder for you. Figure III.17 shows some preference files in the Preferences folder.

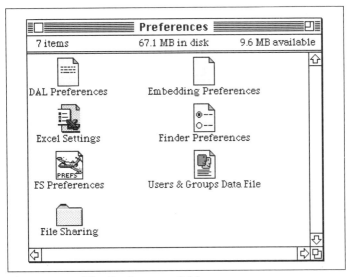

Figure III.17: The Preferences folder

NOTE

If an application places its preference files directly in the System Folder, leave them there, otherwise the application will not be able to find them! Microsoft Word 4.0, for example, stores its preference files directly in the System Folder. The new version of Word stores these files in the Preferences folder.

THE PRINTMONITOR DOCUMENTS FOLDER

This folder stores files to be printed in background. *Background printing* is the printing of documents while you are working on other things. It is managed by the Print-Monitor program.

The PrintMonitor program opens automatically whenever you print a document with background printing turned on. PrintMonitor looks in the System Folder for a PrintMonitor Documents folder and creates one if none exists. PrintMonitor then sends the information to be printed to a file in this folder and returns control of the Mac to you, printing the file slowly while you do other work. Unless a print job is in-process, the PrintMonitor Documents folder is empty.

THE STARTUP ITEMS FOLDER

This folder stores the applications, desk accessories, documents, and folders you want to open automatically when the Macintosh starts up. Be careful when placing a folder in the Startup Items folder, though, as the Macintosh will open *all* items in the folder. If you place more programs in this folder than your computer can hold in memory, the Mac will open as many as it can, displaying a message when it runs out of memory.

 PROCEDURE

To designate startup items, follow these steps:

1. Double-click the System Folder to open it.

2. Select the applications, desk accessories, documents, aliases, or folders you want available at startup.

3. Drag the items' icons to the Startup Items folder. They will open when you restart the computer.

4. To remove an item as a start-up document, drag its icon completely out of the System Folder. The item will not open when you restart the computer.

 **SEE ALSO**

Part V, The File Menu

PART

THE CONTROL PANELS

Control panels are programs that govern many of the Mac's user-interface settings. Previously, you adjusted and personalized your Mac by selecting the *Control Panel* DA from the *Apple* menu. Now, the control panels work just like any other Mac application, and are always available to you through an alias under the *Apple* menu called *Control Panels*.

Some control panels are installed with System 7; others are available from third-party vendors (such as AfterDark, a great screen-saver). System 7 automatically installs control-panel programs that are appropriate for your computer system, with following exceptions:

▲ Color and Monitors are installed only if you have a color or grayscale monitor.

▲ File Sharing Monitor, Sharing Setup, and Users and Groups are installed only if you select file-sharing during installation.

▲ The Network control panel is installed only if you are connected to TokenTalk or Ethernet.

▲ CloseView is never installed automatically. If you want the benefits of a magnified screen, you must drag the CloseView icon from the "Tidbits" disk into the Control Panels folder.

NOTE

Many procedures in Part IV require you to *restart* the Mac. This means choose *Restart* from the *File* menu.

AN OVERVIEW OF THE CONTROL PANELS

Each control panel has its own icon. See Figure IV.1. Here is a list of each control panel and its function.

Use this control panel...	To do this...
Close View	Magnify the screen display.
Color	Specify colors used in highlighting and window borders.

THE CONTROL PANELS

Use this control panel...   *To do this*...

Easy Access   Use the keyboard instead of
                     the mouse. Designed for
                     people who have difficulty
                     using the mouse or
                     keyboard.

File Sharing   View a list of of items you
Monitor   are sharing and see who is
                     using your shared items.
                     See *Part VI, Sharing Files and
                     Programs*, for information
                     on this control panel.

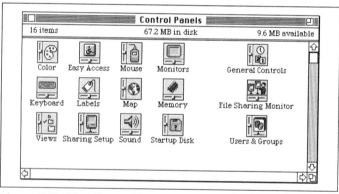

Figure IV.1: The Control Panels folder

Use this control panel...	*To do this...*
General Controls	Set the date and time, change the desktop pattern and color, set the blink rate for the cursor, and control of menus.
Keyboard	Assign international character sets and specify the key-repeat rate and the time delay before repeating.
Labels	Change the colors and names of icon labels.
Map	View the time zone, local time, longitude, and latitude of cities throughout the world.
Memory	Control cache size, virtual memory, and 32-bit addressing options.
Monitors	Designate the main monitor if you are using more than one and set the number of colors or shades of gray that can display.

THE CONTROL PANELS

93

Use this control panel...	To do this...
Mouse	Adjust the double-click speed and the mouse-tracking speed.
Networking	Select the type of networking connection you want. See *Part VI, Sharing Files and Programs.*
Sharing Setup	Identify you and your Mac to the network and turn file-sharing on and off. See *Part VI, Sharing Files and Programs,* for information on this control panel.
Sound	Set speaker volume and choose the alert sound.
Startup Disk	Designate the startup disk if your system has more than one hard disk.
Users and Groups	Register users and groups. See *Part VI, Sharing Files and Programs,* for information on this control panel.

Use this control panel...

To do this...

Views

Customize the icon display by changing the icon's size and display pattern on the desktop, specify what information appears about items in list views, and specify the font and text size displayed in the Finder window.

PROCEDURE

To open a control panel, follow these steps:

1. Choose *Control Panels* from the *Apple* menu.

2. Double-click on a control panel's icon to open it.

NOTE

If there is a control panel that you use frequently, you can place an *alias* of it on the desktop. Make sure you leave the original in the Control Panels folder, though, inside System Folder.

THE CONTROL PANELS

CLOSEVIEW

You can magnify the Macintosh screen and adjust the power of magnification using the *CloseView* control panel. You even have the option of keyboard shortcuts. This control panel is designed to help the visually impaired and is not installed automatically. See Figure IV.2.

 PROCEDURE

To **install CloseView**, follow these steps:

1. Open your System Folder.

2. Open the System 7 "Install 3" disk.

3. Select the CloseView icon and drag it to the Control Panels folder in the System Folder.

4. Restart your computer.

 PROCEDURE

To **select CloseView features**, follow these steps:

1. Open *Control Panels* from the *Apple* menu.

2. Double-click on the CloseView icon to open it.

3. Select the options you want:

▲ To turn CloseView on or off, click the appropriate button in the control panel. Press

Option-⌘-O to turn CloseView on or off from
the keyboard. When CloseView is on, a heavy
frame displays, covering a portion of the screen.

▲ To invert the screen image and display white on
black screen or standard black on white, by
click the appropriate button.

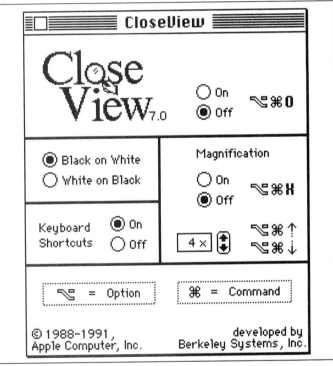

Figure IV.2: CloseView

▲ To turn Keyboard Shortcuts on or off, click On.

▲ To turn Magnification on or off, click the appropriate button in the control panel. When the CloseView frame is displayed, you can turn Magnification on or off by pressing Option-⌘-X.

▲ To adjust the power of magnification, click the up or down arrows in the control panel. On the keyboard, Option-⌘-up arrow increases magnification and Option-⌘-down arrow decreases it.

4. Close the control panel.

COLOR

If your monitor displays grayscales or at least sixteen colors, you can specify the colors of highlighting and window borders. The *highlight* color is the color a selected item changes to.

 PROCEDURE

To color the text highlight, follow these steps:

1. Choose *Control Panels* from the *Apple* menu.

2. Double-click the Color control panel to open it.

3. Choose a color from the Highlight Color pop-up menu. The color will display in the Sample text box. If you want to choose from the color wheel, select *Other...* and the color wheel displays, as shown in Figure IV.3.

4. Place the pointer on the color wheel and click to select the color you want. It will display in the top half of the Color box. The current color displays in the bottom half. If you want to retain the current color, click the lower box.

5. You can change the brightness of the color wheel by dragging the scroll box up or down.

6. When you have found the color you want, click OK.

7. Close the control panel.

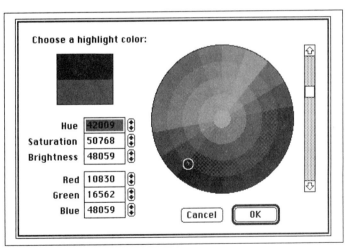

Figure IV.3: The color wheel

PROCEDURE

To color a window's border, follow these steps:

1. Choose the *Control Panels* from the *Apple* menu.

2. Double-click the Color control panel to open it.

3. Choose a color from the Window Color pop-up menu. The color will display in the Sample text box.

4. Close the control panel.

SEE ALSO

▲ *General Controls, "To change the desktop pattern"*

▲ *Labels, "To customize labels"*

▲ *Monitors, "To set the number of colors or grays"*

EASY ACCESS

The *Easy Access* control panel—consisting of three features, Mouse Keys, Slow Keys, and Sticky Keys—is designed for people who have difficulty using the mouse or keyboard. Although you can turn these features on or off from either the control panel or the Finder, it is a good idea to turn on the Use On/Off audio feedback button in the Easy Access window, as shown in Figure IV.4. Then, you hear a whistle whenever you turn an Easy Access feature on or off from the Finder.

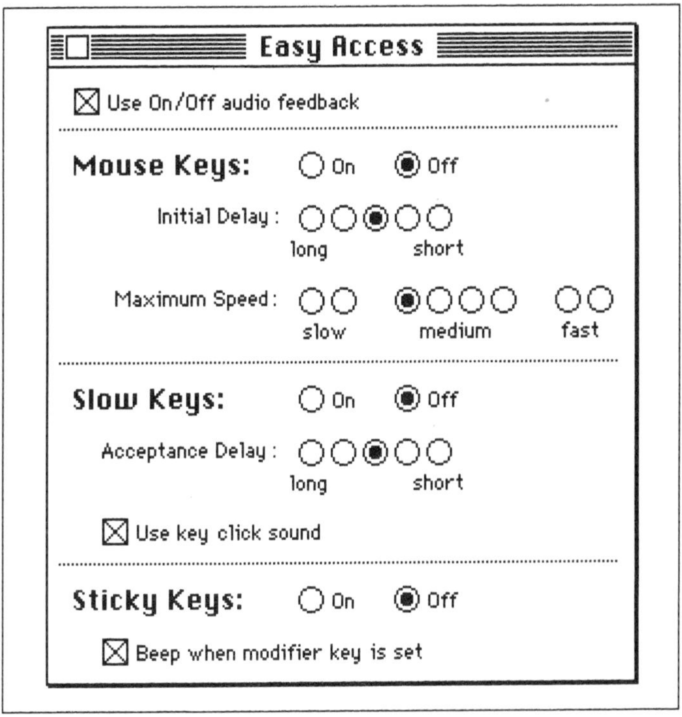

Figure IV.4: Easy Access

Mouse Keys

Mouse Keys lets you move the on-screen pointer using the numeric pad on your keyboard.

PROCEDURE

To use Mouse Keys, follow these steps:

1. Open *Control Panels* from the *Apple* menu.
2. Double-click on the Easy Access icon to open it.
3. Click the appropriate button to turn Mouse Keys on or off and adjust the settings to your liking.
4. Close the control panel.
5. Use the numeric keyboard, as shown, to move the pointer.

The arrows shown indicate the directions the pointer moves when you press a key. Clicking the key once moves the pointer incrementally, holding it down moves the pointer continuously. The 5 key represents the mouse button—press once to click, twice to double-click. Holding down the 0 key locks the mouse button, letting you drag an item with one of the directional keys. The decimal point key or the 5 key unlocks the mouse button.

 KEYBOARD SHORTCUTS

▲ Turn on Mouse Keys by pressing ⌘-Shift-Clear from the Finder.

▲ Turn off Mouse Keys by pressing Clear.

Slow Keys

Slow Keys turns off the the Mac's key repeat feature so you don't accidentally type a string of characters on the screen. It also sets the *acceptance delay*—the length of time that elapses between holding down a key and the resulting action.

THE CONTROL PANELS

PROCEDURE

To use Slow Keys, follow these steps:

1. Open *Control Panels* from the *Apple* menu.

2. Double-click on the Easy Access icon to open it.

3. Turn Slow Keys on or off and set the desired acceptance delay. Click the Use key click sound button to hear an alert signal whenever you press a key.

4. Close the control panel.

 KEYBOARD SHORTCUT

You can turn Slow Keys on or off from the Finder by holding down the Return key for about eight seconds. You'll hear beeps and whistles to confirm.

Sticky Keys

Sticky Keys lets you give two or more *key commands* sequentially instead of simultaneously. These are keystrokes that involve one of the Mac's *modifier keys*. The modifier keys are ⌘, *Option, Shift*, and *Control*.

PROCEDURE

To use Sticky Keys, follow these steps:

1. Open *Control Panels* from the *Apple* menu.

2. Double-click on the Easy Access icon to open it.

3. Turn Sticky Keys on or off. When Sticky Keys goes on, you will hear a whistle and see an icon in the menu bar.

   To hear a beep after you press a modifier key, click the Beep when modifier key is set button.

4. Close the control panel.

   Press the modifier key you want, followed by the keys that complete the command. Notice that the Sticky Keys icon changes, indicating the modifier key has been pressed.

If you press the modifier key twice, it locks. The icon changes again to indicate the modifier key has been locked.

THE CONTROL PANELS

 **KEYBOARD SHORTCUT**

Turn Sticky Keys on or off from the Finder by pressing
the Shift key five times. Don't move the mouse, though,
otherwise you have to start over.

GENERAL
CONTROLS ▲

The *General Controls* control panel, shown in Figure IV.5
should look familiar to Mac users, with one exception.
The RAM-cache options, which used to be in this window, are now accessed in the Memory control panel.

 PROCEDURE

To set the date and time, follow these steps:

1. Choose *Control Panels* from the *Apple* menu.

2. Double-click the General Controls icon to open it.

3. Click either the 12-hour or the 24-hour clock button, depending on which you prefer.

4. To change the hour, minutes, seconds, or meridian,
   click the part of time you want to change. The part is
   highlighted, and up and down arrows display to the

right. Click on arrows until the time you want displays. You can also type a number or letter. Then click the clock icon to save your settings.

5. To change the month, day, or year, click the part of date you want to change. The part is highlighted and up and down arrows display to the right. Click on the arrows until the date you want

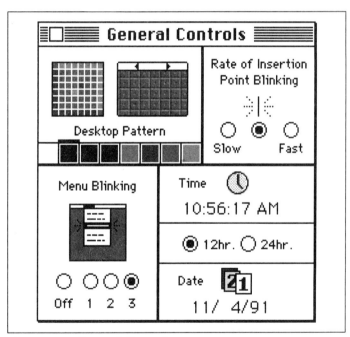

Figure IV.5: General Controls

displays. You can also type a number. Then click the calendar icon to save your settings.

6. Close the control panel.

SEE ALSO

Part III, Using Desk Accessories

Customizing the Desktop

Apple provides you with a variety of desktop patterns. You can even create your own patterns by changing one of the installed ones.

PROCEDURE

To change the Desktop Pattern, follow these steps:

1. Choose *Control Panels* from the *Apple* menu.

2. Double-click the General Controls icon to open it.

3. Click on one of the small triangles at the top of the miniature desktop display, and the variety of available patterns displays, one by one. A magnified view of each pattern displays in the box to the left.

Desktop Pattern

When you find a pattern you like, you can replace the current pattern by clicking the miniature desktop.

4. If you click on a square in the magnified view of the pattern, you change the color or shade of the square. The changes are reflected in the miniature desktop.

5. To change colors, select a color from the color bar and click the square you want to change. If you want to change an existing color, double-click in the color bar and choose a new one from the color wheel.

6. Click the miniature desktop to display the new pattern on your desktop. Double-click the miniature desktop to save the new pattern to reuse it later, otherwise the design is lost.

7. Close the control panel.

 SEE ALSO

▲ Color, "To color the text highlight" and "To color a window's border"

THE CONTROL PANELS

▲ *Monitors, "To set the number of colors or grays"*

The *insertion point* indicates the place in a document where new material will be placed. It is sometimes called the *cursor* when you are working with text.

 PROCEDURE

To adjust the blinking rate of the Insertion Point, follow these steps:

1. Choose *Control Panels* from the *Apple* menu.

2. Double-click the General Controls icon to open it.

3. Click the button you want. The sample insertion point blinks at the selected rate of speed.

4. Close the control panel.

 PROCEDURE

To set the blinking rate of menu items, follow these steps:

1. Choose *Control Panels* from the *Apple* menu.

2. Double-click the General Controls icon to open it.

3. Specify the number of times you want the menu item to blink. Click the Off button to prevent blinking.

4. Close the control panel.

KEYBOARD

The *Keyboard* control panel lets you assign different character sets to your keyboard, specify the repeat rate for keys, and determine the delay before a character begins repeating. It is illustrated in Figure IV.6.

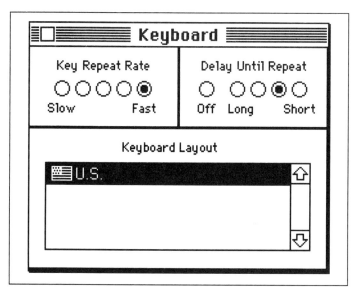

Figure IV.6: The Keyboard control panel

The Keyboard Layout

The character set supplied in the United States is shown in Figure IV.6. You can purchase other character sets from your Apple dealer—British, Deutsche, and Italano, for example.

 PROCEDURE

To select an international character set, follow these steps:

1. Choose *Control Panels* from the *Apple* menu.

2. Double-click the Keyboard control panel to open it.

3. Select the character set you want.

4. Close the control panel.

 NOTE

You can install a keyboard file by dragging its icon inside an open System file.

 PROCEDURE

To specify how fast a character repeats, follow these steps:

1. Choose *Control Panels* from the *Apple* menu.

2. Double-click the Keyboard control panel to open it.

3. Click the Key Repeat Rate button you want.

4. Close the control panel.

Key Repeat Delay

If keys begin to repeat too quickly for your taste, you can adjust the key-repeat delay.

 PROCEDURE

To adjust the key-repeat delay, follow these steps:

1. Choose *Control Panels* from the *Apple* menu.

2. Double-click the Keyboard control panel to open it.

3. Click the Delay Until Repeat button you want. To turn off the key repeat feature altogether, click Off .

4. Close the control panel.

LABELS

The *Labels* controls panel, shown in Figure IV.7, lets you customize label names and specify the colors available for icons. However, you will see colors only if your monitor is set to display at least sixteen colors or gray shades.

THE CONTROL PANELS

A file's label displays when the contents of the Finder window are shown as a list. You can designate label names that are meaningful to you and, if you have a color or grayscale Mac, colors and shades, too. Then, you can use these labels to group files or search for a file using the label name.

 PROCEDURE

To customize labels, follow these steps:

1. Choose *Control Panels* from the *Apple* menu.

2. Double-click on the Labels control panel to open it.

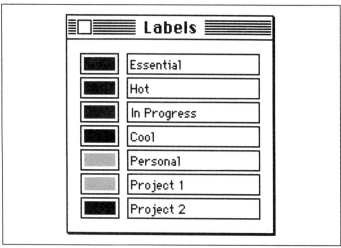

Figure IV.7: The Labels control panel

3. Click the label you want to change.

4. Type the new label.

5. If you have a color or grayscale monitor and want to change the color of the icon, select the color box to the left of the label. The color wheel opens. Place the pointer on the color wheel and click to select a new color. It displays in the top half of the color square. The current color remains displayed in the bottom half. Click OK when you have selected the desired color.

6. Close the control panel.

MAP

The *Map* control panel shows you the locations of many major cities, including latitude, longitude, time zone, and local time. See Figure IV.8.

 PROCEDURE

To locate a city, follow these steps:

1. Choose *Control Panels* from the *Apple* menu.

2. Double-click on the Map control panel to open it.

3. Type the name of a city in the box.

115

4. Click the Find button. The location flashes on the
   map and the city's latitude, longitude, time zone,
   and local time display.

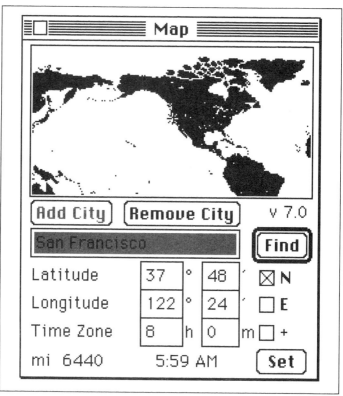

Figure IV.8: The Map

PROCEDURE

To add a city, follow these steps:

1. Choose *Control Panels* from the *Apple* menu.

2. Double-click on the Map control panel to open it.

3. Type the name of a city in the box.

4. Enter the city's latitude and longitude or click on the map to show its general location.

5. Click the Add City button.

6. Close the control panel, and the city will be added to the Map control panel.

 PROCEDURE

To remove a city, follow these steps:

1. Choose *Control Panels* from the *Apple* menu.

2. Double-click on the Map control panel to open it.

3. Choose the city you wish to remove.

4. Click the Remove City button.

5. Close the control panel. The city will be removed from the Map control panel.

THE CONTROL PANELS

MEMORY

Now that MultiFinder is always on, it is easy to exceed the amount of available memory. The *Memory* control panel, shown in Figure IV.9, lets you manage the Mac's available memory with several options: disk cache, virtual memory, and 32-bit addressing. If your Macintosh model can't use virtual memory or 32-bit addressing, these options won't display.

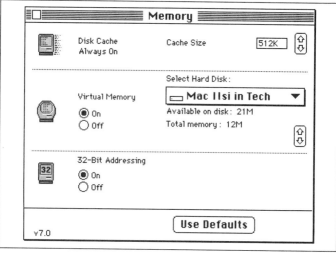

Figure IV.9: The Memory control panel

The *disk cache* is RAM set aside for programs to hold their most recent information. Information can be read from the disk cache much faster than from the disk itself. But there is a trade-off. The larger the disk cache, the fewer programs you can run because there is less available memory. In System 7, disk cache is on all the time. If you find yourself often running out of memory, try setting the disk cache to a smaller size. Be aware, though, that reducing the cache below its default setting can significantly reduce performance. It is probably not a good idea to set to less than 32K for every 1 Mb of installed RAM.

When you turn on *virtual memory*, the system sets aside space on your hard disk and uses it as though it were RAM. However, the hard-disk space used for virtual memory is not available for storing files. Virtual memory is most useful when you are using many programs simultaneously. You will probably notice that all of the Mac's operations take longer when you have virtual memory turned on.

32-bit addressing lets the Mac handle more memory locations, thereby making use of considerably more RAM. With this option turned on, some Macintosh models can use up to 128 Mb of RAM—considerably more if virtual memory is also turned on. Use this option carefully, though; many programs may not be compatible with it.

To use these options effectively, familiarize yourself with the amount of memory your Macintosh has and the memory requirements of the applications you use.

THE CONTROL PANELS

PROCEDURE

To adjust the disk cache, follow these steps:

1. Choose *Control Panels* from the *Apple* menu.

2. Double-click on the Memory control panel to open it.

3. Click the up or down arrow to adjust the size of the disk cache or click Use Defaults to set the disk cache to the preset amount.

4. Close the control panel.

5. Restart the computer. The new disk-cache setting will take effect.

 PROCEDURE

To turn virtual memory on or off, follow these steps:

1. Choose *Control Panels* from the *Apple* menu.

2. Double-click on the Memory control panel to open it.

3. Click the On button to turn on virtual memory.

4. Select the hard disk on which you want to allocate virtual memory. The amount of available space on the selected hard disk displays below the hard disk's pop-up menu.

5. Click the up or down arrows to specify the amount of disk space you want to allocate. The Macintosh puts a VM Storage File on the selected disk equal to the amount of memory you have allocated.

6. Close the control panel.

7. Restart the computer. The new virtual-memory setting will take effect. The total memory now available for application programs includes the disk space you have allocated.

 PROCEDURE

To turn 32-bit addressing on and off, follow these steps:

1. Choose *Control Panels* from the *Apple* menu.

2. Double-click on the Memory control panel to open it.

3. Click the appropriate button to turn 32-bit addressing on or off.

4. Close the control panel.

5. Restart the computer. 32-bit addressing will take effect.

 NOTE

To see the amount of memory available for applications, select *About this Macintosh* under the *Apple* menu.

THE CONTROL PANELS

121

SEE ALSO

▲ *Part V, The Apple Menu*

▲ *Part V, The File Menu*

MONITORS ▲

The *Monitors* control panel, illustrated in Figure IV.10, manages the relationship between multiple monitors. If your monitor can display color or shades of gray, the Monitors control panel lets you set the number of colors or grays that display.

PROCEDURE

To set the number of colors or grays, follow these steps:

1. Choose *Control Panels* from the *Apple* menu.

2. Double-click on the Monitors control panel to open it.

3. Click the monitor icon whose colors you want to set. The icon displays a dark border, showing that it has been selected.

4. Click the Grays or Colors button.

5. Click the number of colors or shades of gray you
   want displayed. (The results, of course, will vary,
   depending on your monitor.) Or, you can click
   Black & White.

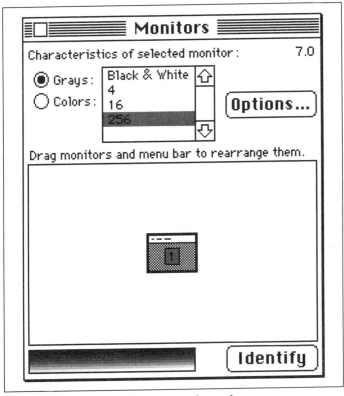

Figure IV.10: The Monitors control panel

6. Close the control panel.

7. Restart your Macintosh.

  SEE ALSO

▲ *Color, "To color the text highlight" and "To change the window's borders"*

▲ *General Controls, "To change the desktop pattern"*

▲ *Part V, The Labels Menu*

Coordinating Your Monitors

You can indicate the relative positions of multiple monitors. If you have more than one monitor, you must specify their relative positions so the pointer can move between them.

  PROCEDURE

To position the monitors, follow these steps:

1. Choose *Control Panels* from the *Apple* menu.

2. Double-click on the Monitors control panel to open it.

3. Click on the Identify or Options... button to view information on each monitor. The Identify button displays the number assigned to each monitor. The Option... button displays the video card the monitor is connected to. The scroll box indicates the number of colors the monitor is set to display.

4. Drag the monitor icon to the position on the screen that corresponds to its actual location. Release the mouse button when the icon is positioned where you want it.

5. Repeat steps 3 and 4 if you have other monitors to position.

6. Close the control panel.

7. Choose *Restart* from the *Special* menu.

The Main Monitor

The main monitor is the one that displays the menu bar and determines the attributes of the screen display. For example, if you have both a black-and-white monitor and a color monitor, with the color one designated as the main monitor, the labels and options will be available on the black-and-white monitor. If the reverse is true, though, neither monitor can take advantage of color options.

PROCEDURE

To designate the main monitor, follow these steps:

1. Choose *Control Panels* from the *Apple* menu.

2. Double-click on the Monitors control panel to open it.

3. Click on the Identify button to view the number assigned to a monitor. The scroll box displays the number of colors the monitor is set to display.

4. Drag the white menu bar to the monitor icon you want as your main monitor. Release the mouse button when the menu bar is positioned where you want it.

5. Close the control panel.

6. Choose *Restart* from the *Special* menu.

MOUSE

Use the *Mouse* control panel to adjust the double-clicking speed of the mouse and the mouse-tracking speed. See Figure IV.11.

The onscreen movement of the pointer can be adjusted to correspond with the movements of the mouse to varying degrees. Try different speeds and find the one that feels right to you. The Very Slow button is a special application for use with *tablets*. Tablets give you pixelar control over pointer movement, which is useful for tasks requiring great precision, such as graphics.

 PROCEDURE

To set mouse-pointer movement, follow these steps:

1. Choose *Control Panels* from the *Apple* menu.

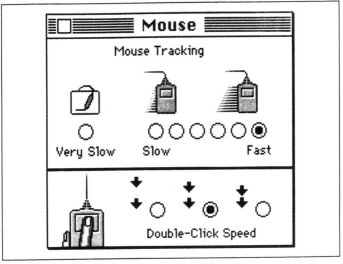

Figure IV.11: The Mouse control panel

2. Double-click the Mouse control panel to open it.

3. Click the button for the speed you want.

4. Close the control panel.

 PROCEDURE

To adjust the double-clicking speed, follow these steps:

1. Choose *Control Panels* from the *Apple* menu.

2. Double-click on the Mouse control panel to open it.

3. Click the double-clicking speed you want. The button beneath the closely spaced arrows is fastest.

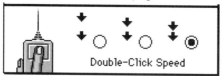

If the Mac is not interpreting your double-clicks accurately, you might want to select a faster speed. If the Mac is interpreting two unrelated clicks as a double-click, try selecting a slower speed.

4. Close the control panel.

SOUND

You use the *Sound* control panel (shown in Figure IV.12) to
set speaker volume and choose the sound the Macintosh

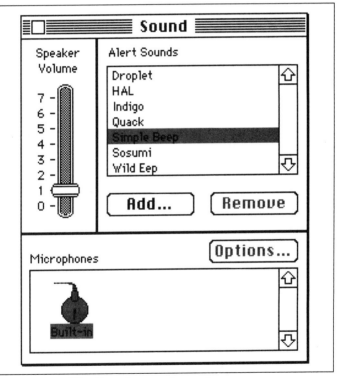

Figure IV.12: The Sound control panel

makes when it signals you (the *alert*). If your Macintosh has a sound-input port, you can connect a microphone and record sounds.

 PROCEDURE

To adjust speaker volume, follow these steps:

1. Choose *Control Panels* from the *Apple* menu.
2. Double-click on the Sound control panel to open it.
3. Select a sound.
4. Drag the speaker's volume bar to set the volume for the Mac's built-in speaker. You can choose one of eight volume settings. If you set the volume to zero, the menu bar flashes instead of making a sound.
5. When you release the mouse button, you will hear the sound at the volume you have selected.
6. Close the control panel.

 PROCEDURE

To select the alert sound, follow these steps:

1. Choose *Control Panels* from the *Apple* menu.
2. Double-click on the Sound control panel to open it.

3. Click the name of the alert sound you want from the displayed list. The sound will play when you click the name.

4. Close the control panel.

PROCEDURE

To record sounds, follow these steps:

1. Be sure your microphone is properly installed and connected to the Macintosh.

2. Choose *Controls Panel* from the *Apple* menu.

3. Double-click on the Sound control panel to open it.

4. Highlight the icon representing the sound-input device you want to use.

5. Click the Add button and a dialog box will appear.

6. Click the Record button. You have ten seconds of recording time.

7. Click Stop when you are finished recording.

THE CONTROL PANELS

8. Click Play to hear the sound you have just recorded.

9. Click Save to save the sound. A regular save dialog box will display.

10. Enter a name for the sound and click OK or hit Return.

11. Close the control panel.

 SEE ALSO

Part III, The System File

STARTUP DISK ▲

If you use more than one hard disk, you must specify which one you want to be the startup disk.

 PROCEDURE

To specify a startup disk, follow these steps:

1. Choose the *Controls Panel* from the *Apple* menu.

2. Double-click the Startup Disk control panel to open it.

3. Figure IV.13 shows two disk icons. Your Startup Disk control panel will display available hard disks. Click the icon of the disk you want to function as the startup.

4. Close the control panel.

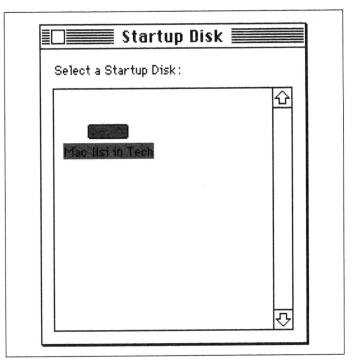

Figure IV.13: Startup Disk

5. Restart the computer. The disk you selected will
display in the top-right corner of the screen, above
any other disks.

VIEWS

The *Views* control panel lets you customize the display of
icons in the Finder window. You can also change the font
or size of text used in Finder windows or on the desktop.
And finally, you can control the amount of information
displayed about each item in a list view window. The
Views control panel is shown in Figure IV.14.

 PROCEDURE

To change the font and size of text in a window, follow
these steps:

1. Choose *Control Panels* from the *Apple* menu.

2. Double-click on the Views control panel to open it.

3. You can change any of the following options:

   ▲ Change the *font* displayed in icon names
   and list views, by clicking on the font name.
   A pop-up menu of fonts currently installed
   in your system file displays. Drag through
   the menu to choose one.

▲ Change the *font size,* by clicking on the triangle next to the box and selecting from the menu of sizes. Or, type a number in the box.

4. Close the control panel.

PROCEDURE

To change icon views, follow these steps:

1. Choose *Control Panels* from the *Apple* menu.

2. Double-click on the Views control panel to open it.

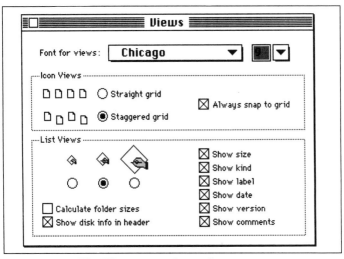

Figure IV.14: The Views control panel

3. You can change any of the following options:

▲ Select the *arrangement* of icons on the desktop by clicking the button adjacent to the desired grid pattern. When you choose the *Clean Up Window* command from the *Special* menu, the icons will be arranged in the pattern selected. If you specify Straight grid, icons display in straight rows. If you select Staggered grid, icons display in staggered layout, which permits more icons in a window without overlapping names.

▲ To force icons to snap to an invisible grid on the desktop, click the box *Always snap to grid* in the Icon Views section. Once this option is selected, the only way to move an icon off the grid point is to hold down ⌘ when you drag the icon.

4. Close the control panel.

 PROCEDURE

To change the information in list views, follow these steps:

1. Choose *Control Panels* from the *Apple* menu.

2. Double-click on the Views control panel to open it.

3. You can change any of the following options:

▲ Select the size you want icons to display in list views by clicking the button beneath the icon you want.

▲ Select which information will display in list views by clicking on the "Show" box options you want. Although the item's name always appears, size, kind, label, date, version and comments can also display, by checking or unchecking the relevant Show box.

▲ Display the *folder size* in the list view window by clicking the *Calculate folder sizes* checkbox. Instead of a dash, you see the total size of the folder and its contents. If you have a lot of folders on your disk, this option can slow down screen response.

▲ Display a disk's available space by clicking the *Show disk info in header* checkbox. The information displays just under a window's title bar. Previously, you had to switch to icon view for this information.

4. Close the control panel.

THE CONTROL PANELS

PART

FINDER

The Finder is an integral part of the system software. It creates the desktop and helps you manage disks, applications, folders, and files. Although the Finder will look the same to experienced Mac users, there are many new features. For example, the Finder menus have a slightly different look.

The following section describes the menus and commands included with the system software. These are pull-down menus. To view the commands available on a menu, point to the menu's name in the menu bar. Click and hold the mouse button to open the menu, then drag the pointer to highlight the command you want. Release the mouse button, and the command will execute. Dimmed commands are not available.

THE APPLE MENU

You can put any kind of file you want to access easily—
desk accessories, documents, folders, aliases—into the
Apple menu.

When you install the system software, the Alarm Clock,
Calculator, Chooser, Control Panels, Key Caps, Note Pad,
Puzzle, and Scrapbook are placed in the Apple Menu
Items folder. Although desk accessories are usually stored
in the Apple Menu Items folder, you can place them
anywhere you find convenient and open them by double-
clicking on their icons. Any items you place in the Apple
Menu Items folder will appear under the *Apple* menu, as
shown in Figure V.1.

Open any item in the Apple Menu Items folder by
choosing its name from the *Apple* menu. The following
section gives you information about the *Apple* menu
options. Refer to *Part IV, The Control Panels* for more information on these items.

> *About This Macintosh*   Displays
> information on available memory
> and current memory allocation. This
> command appears only when you are
> working in the Finder. Choosing
> *About This Macintosh* brings up the
> dialog box shown in Figure V.2.

THE FINDER

Alarm Clock Lets you set an alarm to sound at a time you specify.

 Calculator Works as a four-function pocket calculator.

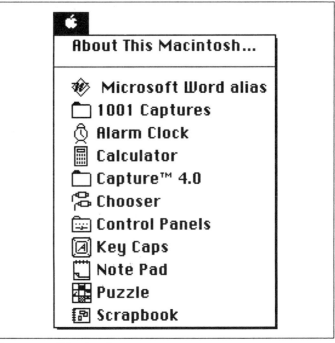

Figure V.1: The Apple menu

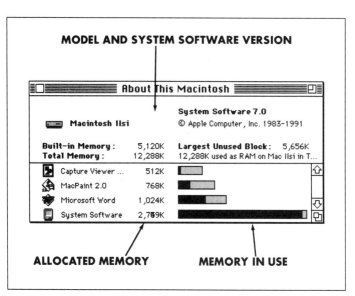

Chooser Lets you select a printer or other device. If you are attached to a network, you can select disks and printers available on the network.

Control Panels Lets you customize your system.

Key Caps Shows the location of characters for each font installed in the System file.

MODEL AND SYSTEM SOFTWARE VERSION

About This Macintosh

System Software 7.0
© Apple Computer, Inc. 1983-1991

Macintosh IIsi

| Built-in Memory : | 5,120K | **Largest Unused Block :** 5,656K |
| Total Memory : | 12,288K | 12,288K used as RAM on Mac IIsi in T... |

Capture Viewer ...	512K	
MacPaint 2.0	768K	
Microsoft Word	1,024K	
System Software	2,759K	

ALLOCATED MEMORY   **MEMORY IN USE**

THE FINDER

Figure V.2: About This Macintosh

Note Pad   Stores small amounts of information. Useful for jotting down notes while you're working on something else.

 The Puzzle   Takes your mind off serious matters for a little while.

 Scrapbook   Saves text or graphics that you have cut or copied. The scrapbook can store multiple items which you can paste into documents. You can view items stored in the scrapbook by choosing it from the *Apple* menu.

 SEE ALSO

▲ *Part III, The Apple Menu Items Folder*

▲ *Part IV, An Overview of the Control Panels*

▲ *The Edit Menu*

▲ *Part VI, Sharing Files and Programs*

THE FILE MENU

There are significant changes to the Finder's *File* menu. The following section discusses each command in the *File* menu, shown in Figure V.3. If there is a keyboard shortcut, it is shown to the right of the command.

File	
New Folder	⌘N
Open	⌘O
Print	⌘P
Close Window	⌘W
Get Info	⌘I
Sharing...	
Duplicate	⌘D
Make Alias	
Put Away	⌘Y
Find...	⌘F
Find Again	⌘G
Page Setup...	
Print Window...	

Figure V.3: The File menu

⌘-N   *New Folder* Creates an empty folder when you're working in a Finder window or on the desktop. A folder icon appears named *untitled folder*. The name will be selected, so you can type a new folder name if you want to. Deselect the folder by pressing Return or clicking anywhere outside the folder icon.

⌘-O   *Open* Opens the selected document, folder, or application. The selected icon opens into a window. Note that if you are working in an application, choosing *Open...* from the *File* menu displays the application's directory dialog box.

⌘-P   *Print* Prints files directly from the Finder. Select the files you want to print. Then select the print options you want in the print dialog box, as shown in Figure V.4. Click the Print button or press Return. You can select a single file or several files created by different applications. A separate print dialog box displays for each application.

⌘-W   *Close Window* Replaces the old *Close* command and functions the same way. This command works the same as clicking on the active window's close box (the small box in the upper-left corner)—it closes, displaying its icon, which remains selected.

⌘-I   *Get Info* Displays information about a single item on the desktop or in a Finder window.

⌘-D   *Duplicate* Makes a duplicate of a selected item on the same disk. If you duplicate a folder, the items in the folder are included in the duplicate copy. A duplicate is named with the name of the original followed by *copy*.

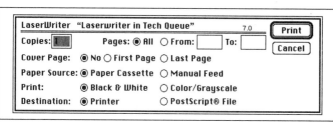

LaserWriter	"Laserwriter in Tech Queue"	7.0

Copies: [1]   Pages: ◉ All ○ From: [ ] To: [ ] [**Print**] [Cancel]

Cover Page: ◉ No ○ First Page ○ Last Page

Paper Source: ◉ Paper Cassette ○ Manual Feed

Print: ◉ Black & White ○ Color/Grayscale

Destination: ◉ Printer ○ PostScript® File

Figure V.4: A print dialog box

THE FINDER

Make Alias...   Creates a file you can use as a stand-in for an original file. It is not a copy of the original item. If you open an alias for an application, the original application opens. An alias lets you keep a frequently used file in a convenient location without having to move the original.

⌘-Y   *Put Away*   If you have dragged programs, files, or folders onto the desktop, returns them to their original locations. Select the items and choose *Put Away* from the *File* menu. You can eject a disk by selecting its icon and choosing *Put Away*.

⌘-F   *Find...*   Helps you locate files.

⌘-G   *Find Again*   Reruns the *Find* command, locating and displaying the next item matching the criteria you have specified in the *Find...* command. If the Mac cannot find an item that meets the search criteria, an alert sounds.

Page Setup... Sets up the page size, orientation, and other options for documents that you print in the Finder, as shown in Figure V.5. Once selected, the options remain in effect until you change them. Please note that these selections apply only to printing from the Finder.

Print Window... Prints the actual contents of the active window, in any view, including items not visible on the screen. Simply choose the command and then click Print.

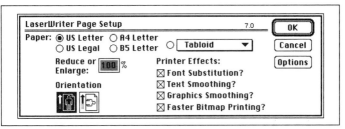

Figure V.5: The Page Setup dialog box

THE FINDER

A Few Tips on Printing

As different printers offer different print options, consult your printer's documentation for detailed information.

If you have background printing turned on, you can control the printing operation with PrintMonitor, which comes with the system software. Once a document starts printing, choose *PrintMonitor* from the *Application* menu. Select the options you want, and click the close box. You can cancel printing, take documents out of the print queue, set the time you want a document to print, or postpone a print job indefinitely. PrintMonitor also keeps you posted on the status of the print job. For example, it tells you how many pages have been printed, how many are still waiting to print, whether the printer has paper, and so on.

Using Get Info

The Get Info dialog box provides you with a wealth of useful information concerning the file or application you have selected.

Viewing Information

Select an application, document, alias, folder, or disk and choose the *Get Info* command from the *File* menu. A dialog box displays showing information about the selected item and offering some options. A somewhat different dialog box displays for each different kind of file. Figure V.6 is an example of the Get Info dialog box.

```
┌──────────────────────────────────────────┐
│  ▤□▤▤  Microsoft Word Info  ▤▤▤          │
│                                            │
│    W    Microsoft Word                     │
│         Microsoft Word 4.0                 │
│                                            │
│    Kind : application program              │
│    Size : 669K on disk (683,287 bytes used)│
│                                            │
│   Where : Mac IIsi in Tech : Applications :│
│           Microsoft Word 4.0 :             │
│                                            │
│  Created : Mon, Apr 10, 1989, 5:00 PM      │
│ Modified : Tue, Oct 22, 1991, 4:20 PM      │
│  Version : 4.0, © 1987-1989 Microsoft      │
│            Corporation                     │
│ Comments :                                 │
│  ┌──────────────────────────────────────┐ │
│  │                                       │ │
│  │                                       │ │
│  └──────────────────────────────────────┘ │
│            ┌─Memory─────────────────┐      │
│            │ Suggested size : 512  K │      │
│ ☐ Locked  │ Current size : 1024  K │      │
│            └────────────────────────┘      │
└──────────────────────────────────────────┘
```

Figure V.6: The Get Info dialog box

THE FINDER

The following information displays in the dialog box: the item's *name,* as it appears on the desktop, its *icon, kind* (application, alias, document, folder, disk), *size* (the amount of space it uses on disk), *where* (its location), *created* (date and time it was created), *modified* (the date and time it was last changed), and *version* (for documents and programs).

 PROCEDURE

To add comments, enter text in the Comments: box at the bottom of the Get Info dialog box. Comments are an additional file management tool, as they can specify a file's contents. Comments can even be displayed in Finder windows if you activate the *Show Comments* option in the Views control panel. Plus, you can search for files using comment text. For example, if you type a project name in the Comments: box, you can search for the project's files using the *Find...* command or list them *by Comments* from the *View* menu.

 **SEE ALSO**

Part IV, Views

Customizing an Icon

System 7 lets you replace a program's standard icon with a graphic in the Get Info dialog box. You can copy any icon that catches your fancy or create one using graphic software.

 PROCEDURE

To customize an icon, follow these steps:

1. Select the graphic you want to use and copy it to the Clipboard.

2. Go to the Finder and select the item whose icon you want to change.

3. Choose *Get Info* from the *File* menu and click on the icon in the Get Info window. A box displays around the icon.

If a box doesn't display, you cannot replace this particular icon.

4. Choose *Paste* from the *Edit* menu. The stored graphic replaces the old icon—scaled to the appropriate size.

5. Close the dialog box.

Creating Document Templates

You can turn a data file into a *stationery pad* or *document template* using the *Get Info* command. A template is a file with certain settings—margins, fonts, and text spacing, for instance—that you use repeatedly. Creating such a file saves you the trouble of resetting the format each time you start a new document. Several applications already have this feature, but now System 7 makes the stationery pad available for all applications.

 PROCEDURE

To create a document template, follow these steps:

1. Select the document's icon and choose the *Get Info* command from the *File* menu.

2. Click the Stationery pad box at the bottom of the window. The document icon changes into the stationery pad icon.

3. Close the dialog box.

Notice that the Kind information reflects the change. When you open a stationery pad, you will see a dialog box asking you to name the new document. Save the document under a new name and then open it just as you would any file. The original stationery pad remains as you created it.

Finding the Original File for an Alias

If you select an alias icon and choose *Get Info* from the *File* menu, you get a slightly different window, as seen in Figure V.7. From here, you can locate the file that the alias represents.

 PROCEDURE

To locate the original file, click the Find Original button. The original file will appear on the desktop. The location and file name of the original file appear after the word *Original.*

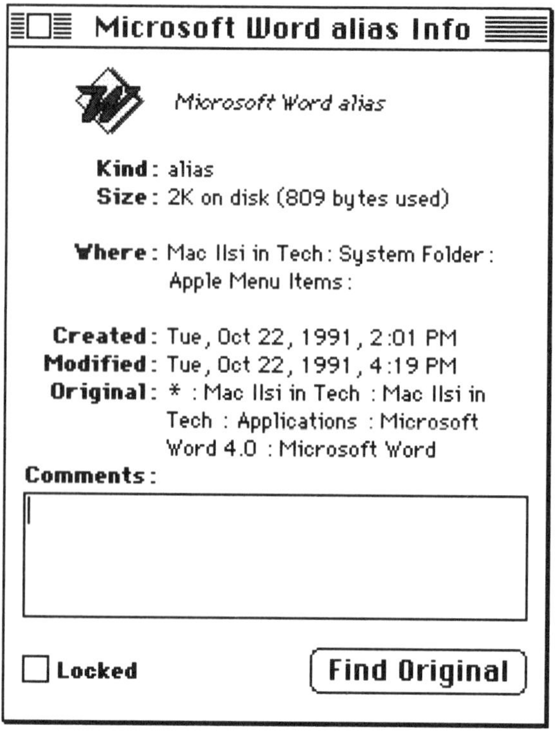

Figure V.7: An alias Get Info window

Changing an Application's Memory Allocation

You can change an application's *memory allocation*. This is the amount of RAM set aside for an application. You might want to increase the allotted memory if you are going to use large files, or decrease it if you plan to open a lot of applications simultaneously. Decreasing the allocation can make an application work slowly, though. In either case, proceed cautiously.

 PROCEDURE

To change an application's memory allocation, follow these steps:

1. Select an application by clicking its icon.

2. Choose *Get Info* from the *File* menu. Notice that, in the Memory section at the bottom of the Get Info dialog box, a suggested amount of memory is listed. The Current size: is the amount of memory the application is currently allotted.

THE FINDER

3. Type a new number in the Current size: box.

4. Close the dialog box.

Protecting Files and Programs

You can protect individual documents, aliases, and applications from change by locking them. You cannot lock a folder, but you can lock all its files. Locking an alias prevents it from being accidentally discarded but does not lock the original file.

PROCEDURE

To lock items, follow these steps:

1. Select the item you want to protect.

2. Choose *Get Info* from the *File* menu.

3. When the Get Info dialog box opens, click the Locked box in the lower-left corner.

☒ **Locked**

4. Close the dialog box.

The information in a locked document or application cannot be changed or thrown away. To discard a locked item, you must first deselect the Locked box. Or you can drag a locked item to the Trash and select the *Empty Trash* command from the *Special* menu while holding down the Option key.

 NOTE

You can turn off the Trash Can alert dialog box by selecting the Trash Can icon, choosing *Get Info* from the *File* menu, and clicking the Warn before emptying box.

 **SEE ALSO**

The Special Menu

Sharing Files and Programs

If you have turned on file-sharing, you can use the *Sharing* command to designate the type of access you want to give to a folder. Then, you can specify the users or groups you want to share folders with and assign their passwords and access privileges.

THE FINDER

SEE ALSO

Part VI, Sharing Files and Programs

Using Aliases

Since aliases take up very little disk space, you can make as many as you like for the same item and place them in different locations in your system. The following are possible uses for aliases:

▲ Putting an alias of an application in the Apple Menu Items folder or on the desktop, so you can launch it without digging through several levels of folders.

▲ Making an alias of a folder that is stored within another folder. Then dragging a file into the alias folder places the file in the original folder.

▲ Creating aliases of files located on floppy disks, removable hard drives, CD-ROMs, and file servers. When you open an alias of a file on a floppy disk, for example, the Mac tells you to insert the disk that contains the original file. This helps you connect to the floppy disk you want! If the original is on a file server, the alias serves as an automatic server connection.

▲ Designating a startup item by making an alias of a document, application, or DA and putting it in the Startup Items folder.

▲ Putting an alias of the Control Panels folder on the desktop if you are frequently opening it to make changes. System 7 places an alias of the Control Panels folder in the Apple Menu Items folder for you.

 PROCEDURE

To make an alias, follow these steps:

1. Select an item in a Finder window.

2. Choose the *Make Alias* command from the *File* menu. An alias icon will appear.

Quicken 1.5 alias

The icon is the same as the original, but the name appears in italics with *alias* added to help you distinguish it from the original file.

3. Move the alias where you want it to go.

You can perform the same operations on an alias that you can on standard files. Renaming the alias file or repositioning it does not break the link to the original file. You can rename and reposition the original file (as long as you do not move it to another disk) without disturbing the

THE FINDER

link to the alias. However, if you discard an original file, you'll find that you can no longer open its aliases. If you don't remember where an original is, select the alias icon, choose *Get Info*, and click the Find Original button.

 SEE ALSO

▲ *Part IV, The Control Panels*

▲ *Part VI, Sharing Files and Programs*

Using the New Find... Command

The *Find...* command has been both improved and expanded. You can

▲ Use *Find...* to search for an item by name.

▲ Use the expanded Find dialog box (shown in Figure V.8) to set criteria for seaching through your files.

▲ Conduct a two-stage search that uses different sets of criteria. This is a useful technique for narrowing down your results if an initial search retrieves a great number of files.

PROCEDURE

To search for a file by name, follow these steps:

1. Choose the *Find...* command from the *File* menu. The Find dialog box appears.

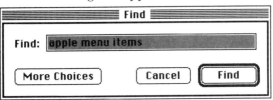

2. Type all or part of the lost file's name (up to 31 characters) into the box and click Find. The Mac searches all the disks and shared folders on your

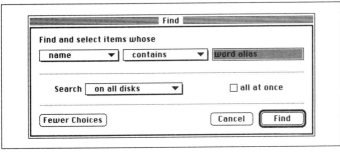

Figure V.8: The expanded Find dialog box

THE FINDER

desktop for file names including the characters you have specified. If no items matching the search criteria are found, you hear an alert sound. The first item found that matches the search criteria is displayed in an open window.

3. To display other items meeting the search criteria, choose the *Find Again* command from the *File* command (⌘-G). The next file that matches the search criteria is located, a window opens, and the file displays.

You can use the search parameters in the Find dialog box until you change them.

PROCEDURE

To search for a file using the expanded Find dialog box, follow these steps:

1. Click the More Choices button. The Find file options dialog box displays.

2. You can search for only one criterion at a time. Specify the criterion to search for, where to search, and how to display the results.

3. Specify the search parameters you want, then click the Find button. If you have selected the *all at once* option, all the files meeting the criterion will be displayed as a list.

- **Raw Sybex**
  - 📁 11.screens
  - 📁 more screens
  - 📄 outline
  - 📄 Picture 5
  - 📁 screen shots
  - ◼ **sybex title profile**

You might have to scroll to see all the found selections. If you have not checked *all at once,* the first result displays, highlighted. To display the rest, you must choose the *Find Again* command or use the keyboard shortcut, ⌘-**G**.

PROCEDURE

To conduct a two-stage search, follow these steps:

1. Choose *Find...* from the *File* menu.

2. When the Find dialog box displays, click the More Choices button.

3. Select the *all at once* box and click the Find button. The found items display in list view.

4. With the found items highlighted, choose the *Find...* command again.

5. Specify another set of search criteria from the expanded Find dialog box.

THE FINDER

6. Choose the *selected items* from the *Search* pop-up menu.

7. Click the Find button.

 NOTE

You can return to the original Find dialog box by clicking the Fewer Choices button.

Expanded Search Options

The following section describes the expanded search options.

▲ Open the left pop-up menu to choose the search criteria. You can search by many criteria—name, creation date, modification date, size, label, kind, comments, version, or lock status. The item selected in the left pop-up menu determines the options available to you in the other menus.

▲ Open the middle pop-up menu to choose the item you want. The menu selections vary depending on what you selected in the left pop-up menu.

▲ Specify the date, choose an item, or enter search text in the right area. The items you have selected in the preceding pop-up menus determine the options available in this area.

▲ Choose a search location from the pop-up menu labeled *Search*. You can search all disks, a specific disk, the active Finder window, or selected items.

▲ Click the box labeled *all at once* to display the found items in a list view.

THE EDIT MENU ▲

Use the Finder's *Edit* menu, shown in Figure V.9, to edit the names of disks, applications, files, and folders. You cannot use the *Edit* menu to discard (cut) or copy icons. If there is a keyboard shortcut for a command, it displays to the right. Please note that although you might see an *Edit* menu when you are using an application, the commands will vary. This section describes some fundamental operations common to *all* applications. These operations include copying, moving, deleting, and storing text and images.

Here is a descriptive list of each command.

⌘-Z *Undo* Reverses an action. If it is not possible to reverse the action, the *Undo* command is dimmed. Often it is possible to undo an undo.

THE FINDER

⌘X *Cut* Deletes text and graphics from
an open document. The deleted item
is stored in the Clipboard and remains
there until you copy or cut another
item. You can use the *Paste* command
to insert the item in a different place
in the same document, in another
document, or even in another
program.

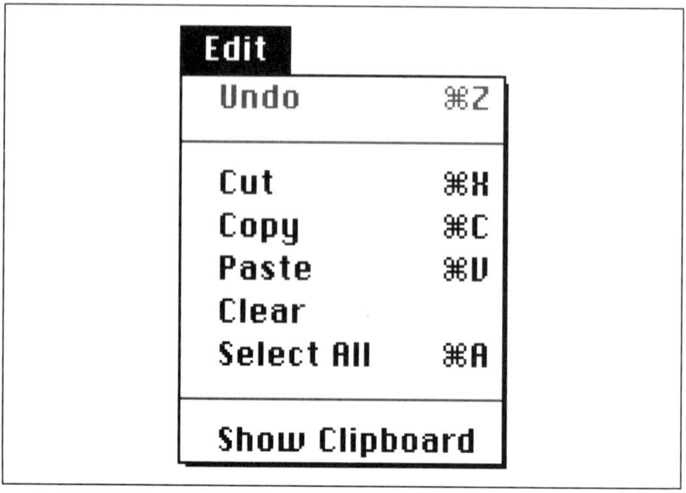

Figure V.9: The Edit menu

⌘-C *Copy* Copies text and graphics from an open document. The item is stored in the Clipboard and remains there until you copy or cut another item. You can use the *Paste* command to insert the item in a different place in the same document, in another document, or even in another program.

⌘-V *Paste* Places text and graphics stored in the Clipboard in an open document. You can continue to paste the item until you cut or copy a new selection.

Clear Deletes text and graphics from an open document. The item is *permanently* discarded and cannot be replaced because the material is not placed on the Clipboard. Clearing items does not disturb the contents of the Clipboard. You can also clear selected items by pressing the Delete key.

⌘-A *Select All* Selects all icons in the active window or desktop.

Show Clipboard Shows the contents of the Clipboard. This command is available from the Finder and some application programs.

THE FINDER

169

Publish and Subscribe

Publishing and Subscribing is a new and powerful feature of System 7. Only applications that have been designed to make use of this feature will display the *Publish* and *Subscribe* commands on the *Edit* menu. These commands let you create links between documents and update the information automatically or manually. You can update the information on your computer or across a network.

Here's how it works! You designate the material you want to have updated automatically. The material is saved in a special file called an *edition*. Edition file icons display a small shaded rectangle icon on the Finder window.

Solver Edition 2

The material saved in the edition file can be inserted in another file, which is called a *subscriber*. You can make as many subscribers as you want, and they can be on another disk or on a network file-server.

Whenever you change the *publisher* (the original version of the material), the changes will be automatically reflected in the edition file and all subscriber files.

The following procedures are intended to give you an idea of how this exciting new feature works. Each application puts its own twist on things, though, so it is a good

idea to consult an application's documentation before
using publish and subscribe.

 PROCEDURE

To create a publisher, follow these steps:

1. Select the material you want to publish. In our
example, it is a Microsoft Excel chart.

2. Choose *Create Publisher* from the *Edit* menu. The
Mac saves the material in a separate file called an
edition.

3. Name the edition file and save it in any location
you like. The Edition dialog box is shown in Figure V.10.

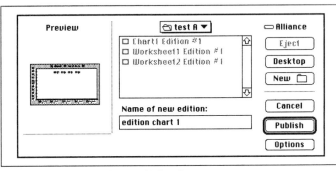

Figure V.10: The Edition dialog box

THE FINDER

4. Click the Publish button. The selected material becomes a *publisher.* Published material might have a light border around it.

When you double-click on the publisher material in the document a Publisher Options dialog box displays. You can view the location of the edition by clicking the *Publisher To* pop-up menu.

You also can specify when you want the subscribers updated. If you do not want the material to be updated automatically, you can cancel the publisher or select the manual updating option.

Once you remove the link between a publisher and an edition file (by clicking the Cancel Publisher button), it cannot be re-established. The subscribed material remains unchanged, but it can no longer be updated.

 NOTE

You cannot work on the edition file directly. You can open an edition file and view its contents by double-clicking its icon. To edit the edition file, click the Open Publisher button as shown in Figure V.11. The publisher document opens, allowing you to make whatever changes you want.

PROCEDURE

To create a subscriber, follow these steps:

1. Open the document where you want to insert the edition.

2. Click on the exact place in the document where you want the material to appear.

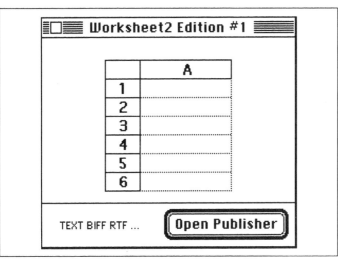

Figure V.11: The Open Publisher button

3. Choose *Subscribe to...* from the *Edit* menu. A dialog box displays as shown in Figure V.12, showing the available edition files.

4. Select the edition file you want.

5. Click the Subscribe button. The edition's material is inserted in the document. Subscribed material might have a dark border around it.

If you double-click on the subscriber material in the document a Subscriber Options dialog box displays. Here you can view the location of the edition by clicking on the *Subscriber To:* pop-up menu. You can also open the publisher and edit the material, specify when you want

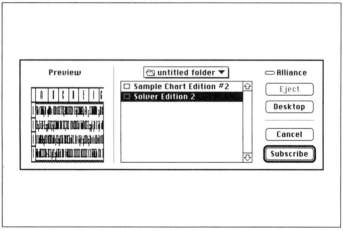

Figure V.12: The Subscribe dialog box

the edition updated, or cancel the link between the sub-scriber and the edition file.

The subscriber material remains in the document and can be updated—either manually or automatically—until you cancel the link to the publisher or delete the publisher itself.

THE VIEW MENU

The *View* menu (see Figure V.13) lets you customize how the contents of a disk or folder are displayed. You can view items by icon or in a list. Viewing items by icon is useful for selecting and moving them. Viewing items in a list is useful when a particular aspect of the item (name, size,

> **View**
> by Small Icon
> ✓ by Icon
> by Name
> by Size
> by Kind
> by Label
> by Date

Figure V.13: The View menu

THE FINDER

175

kind, label, date, etc.) contains important information.
You can easily select items in different folders when you
display the contents of a window in list.

  PROCEDURE

To select a view, pull down the *View* menu and drag to
choose the view you want.

Mac with a View

The following section describes each view in detail. The
particular view that you select determines the *order* in
which files display in the window.

▲ *By Small Icon*   Displays the contents of the active
   window as small icons, letting you see more icons
   in the window.

▲ *By Icon*   Displays the contents of the active window
   as icons.

▲ *By Name*   Displays the contents of the active window in a list, sorted alphabetically by name.

▲ *By Size*   Displays the contents of the active window
   in a list, sorted by size from largest to smallest.
   This option is useful for seeing which items are
   taking up the most space. If you have selected *Cal-*
   culate folder sizes in the Views control panel, folders

are displayed by size as well. Otherwise, they are grouped at the end of the list, alphabetically.

▲ *By Kind*   Displays the contents of the active window in a list, sorted alphabetically by kind. Examples of *kind* include *alias, application, file, folder, system extension,* and *desk accessory.*

▲ *By Label*   Displays the contents of the active window in a list, sorted by the labels you have assigned to them. They display in the same order as they appear in the *Label* menu. Unlabeled files are grouped at the end of the listing.

▲ *By Date*   Displays the contents of the active window in a list, sorted by the date they were last modified. The modification date refers to when you created or changed a file's contents. The most recently modified files display first.

▲ *By Version*   Software developers always assign *version numbers* to their applications. Displays the contents of the active window in a list, sorted by version number, the lowest displaying first.

▲ *By Comment*   Displays the contents of the active window in a list, sorted alphabetically by the text contained in the Get Info dialog box's Comment: field. Files without comments are grouped at the top of the list.

If the contents of a window are displayed as a list, you can change to a different list view without using the *View* menu.

PROCEDURE

To change list views, click the type of view you want at the top of the window. For example, you can click on the *Kind* title to sort files alphabetically by file type, as shown in Figure V.14. Notice that the selected title is underlined.

PROCEDURE

To view the contents of a folder, click the triangle next to a folder name. The contents appear in a list.

▷   🗀 Apple Menu Items
▽   🗀 Control Panels
          🗋 Capture
          🗋 Easy Access
          🗋 Map
          🗋 Views
          🗋 Labels
          🗋 Memory
          🗋 Color
          🗋 File Sharing Monitor
          🗋 General Controls
          🗋 Keyboard
          🗋 Monitors
          🗋 Mouse

The folder's contents display when the triangle faces down, but do not display when the triangle faces right.

When you display the contents of a window as a list, you can move to and open items stored deep inside folders without opening their parent folders. Hierarchical views allow you to select and manipulate files and folders from different levels at the same time.

 PROCEDURE

To select files and folders at multiple levels of the hierarchy, hold down the shift key while selecting the file icons. Then, you can copy, move, or discard them.

CLICK HERE TO DISPLAY ITEMS BY KIND

Name	Size	Kind	Label	Last I
Calendar Creator 1.01	440K	application program	—	Wed, I
PageMaker 4.0	1,523K	application program	—	Tue, F
PowerPoint	409K	application program	—	Wed, I
TeachText	36K	application program	—	Thu, F
Word 4.0	668K	application program	Hot	Tue, S
5.4	1K	Capture Viewer 2....	—	Sat, M
MacDraw II Options	5K	MacDraw II 1.1 do...	—	Wed, I
PM4 Defaults	4K	PageMaker 4.0 doc...	—	Mon, :
FINDER	4K	Word 4.0 document	—	Sun, S

THE FINDER

Figure V.14: A list view

PROCEDURE

To copy a file to another disk, drag the file icon. Background copying lets you copy files while continuing other work. While working within an application, activate the Finder by clicking on the Desktop or selecting *Finder* from the *Application* menu. Drag the selected files from their source location to the icon of the destination folder. When the copy dialog box appears, switch back to the application and resume your work. The Finder will continue to copy in the background.

 PROCEDURE

To move a file or folder to another open window, drag the file or folder icon. Dragging a file to another disk copies it.

 PROCEDURE

To open a file, folder, or application, double-click on its icon. The file, folder, or application opens in a new window, which becomes the active window.

NOTE

The selections you make in the Views control panel affect the commands that display in the *View* menu. Here are some examples:

▲ If you deselect the *Show label* option, the *by Label* command does not display in the *View* menu.

▲ The size of a folder's contents displays in list views if you have selected the *Calculate folder size* option. The trade-off is a considerably slower display speed, depending on your Mac.

▲ The size of a folder's contents displays if you select *Show disk info in header.*

 KEYBOARD SHORTCUTS

To display the contents of a folder, select it from a list and press ⌘-right arrow. ⌘-left arrow closes the expanded display.

 SEE ALSO

Part IV, Views

THE FINDER

THE LABEL MENU ▲

The *Label* menu (shown in Figure V.15) provides an additional way to categorize files and folders. If you have a color or grayscale monitor, you can also assign each label a color—like color-coding your files.

Labels are an easy way to group related files together. You can list a window's contents by label. If you have a color monitor, you can easily identify related icons by assigning a color to each label. In addition, the new *Find...* command lets you use a label as part of your search criteria.

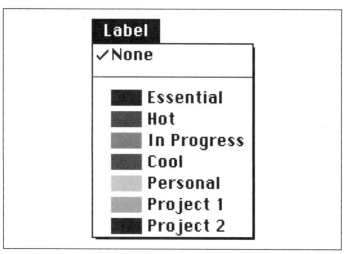

Figure V.15: The Label menu

PROCEDURE

To add a label to an icon, select the icon and choose the label you want from the *Label* menu. The label is visible only when the contents of a window are displayed as a list.

NOTE

You can change the names of labels in the Labels Control Panel. If you have a color or grayscale monitor, you can also set the colors displayed in the *Label* menu in the Labels control panel.

SEE ALSO

▲ *Part IV, Labels*

▲ *Using the New Find… Command*

THE SPECIAL MENU

▲

THE FINDER

The *Special* menu is shown in Figure V.16.

Here is a brief description of each command:

Clean Up Window Rearranges icons on the desktop or in a Finder window. This command is dimmed for items displayed in a list view.

Empty Trash... Deletes all items in the Trash. In System 7, the Trash is no longer automatically emptied.

Eject Disk There are three methods for ejecting disks.

1. Select the disk icon and choose *Eject Disk* from the *Special* menu (⌘-E).
2. Drag the disk icon to the Trash icon.
3. Select the disk icon and choose *Put Away* from the *File* menu (⌘-Y).

Figure V.16: The Special menu

Erase Disk... Erases either a hard disk or a floppy disk. Select the icon of the disk you want to erase. Then, choose *Erase Disk...* from the *Special* menu. Click Initialize or the button representing the disk capacity you want. The disk is erased and reinitialized.

Restart Restarts the Mac.

Shutdown Turns off your Mac. Although the procedure for turning off your computer varies according to model, you should make a habit of using the *Shutdown* command before turning off the power switch. Otherwise, you can damage information.

  PROCEDURE

To throw away an item, follow these steps:

1. Select the item.

2. Drag the item to the Trash icon.

3. When the Trash icon is highlighted, release the mouse button. The Trash icon will bulge, showing there's something inside it.

4. To permanently discard the item, choose *Empty Trash...* from the *Special* menu. An alert box will display. It reports on the contents of the Trash and asks you to confirm that you want to discard them.

5. Click OK to empty the trash or Cancel to stop the operation.

THE FINDER

185

To turn off the warning message, select the Trash icon and choose *Get Info* from the *File* menu. Click the box at the lower-left corner of the window and close the window. Items in the Trash will be discarded without warning when you choose the *Empty Trash...* command. Repeat this procedure to turn the warning back on.

 **SEE ALSO**

Part IV, Views

THE HELP MENU ▲

The question mark icon represents the Help menu.

When you click on this icon, the *Help* menu appears, as shown in Figure V.17.

You can turn on Help information at any time—it is available from the Finder or any application program. When Help is turned on, a "balloon" will appear next to any item you are pointing to.

Microsoft Word

> This is an application—a program with which you can perform a task or create a document. Applications include word processors, graphics programs, database programs, games, and spreadsheets.
>
> Change the icon's name by clicking on the name and typing.

?
About Balloon Help...
Show Balloons
Finder Shortcuts

Figure V.17: The Help menu

THE FINDER

187

The Help menu also provides a summary of keyboard shortcuts for working in the Finder.

Here is a summary of Help functions:

▲ To turn on Help information, choose *Show Balloons* from the *Help* menu.

▲ To turn off Help information, choose *Hide Balloons* from the *Help* menu.

▲ To view a list of Finder shortcuts, choose *Finder Shortcuts* from the *Help* menu.

 NOTE

Not all applications fully utilize System 7's Help facility.

THE APPLICATION MENU

The *Application* menu always appears on the far right of

the menu bar. When you are in the Finder, the Macintosh icon represents the *Application* menu.

MultiFinder lets you open as many applications simultaneously as your Mac's memory permits. Each application you open is added to the *Application*

menu, with the icon of the active application replacing the Macintosh icon. The Finder itself remains available at all times and is listed on the menu. To find out which applications are open, open the *Application* menu and view the list, which is illustrated in Figure V.18.

Clicking on an application's desktop display or selecting its name from the *Application* menu activates it. A checkmark denotes the active application. You can control which applications display on the desktop by choosing the *Hide* and *Show* commands.

You can clean up the clutter of multiple open windows by choosing the *Hide* command from the *Application* menu. When an application is hidden, it continues to operate and can perform tasks in the background. The application icon appears dimmed in the *Application* menu.

Figure V.18: The Application menu

THE FINDER

Hide Others removes all windows from the screen except those of the current application. All open application icons, except that of the current one appear dimmed in the *Application* menu.

Show All displays all open windows.

 NOTE

You can hide a current application when you activate another application. To do this, hold down the Option key and click on the new application's icon or choose it from the *Application* menu.

PART

SHARING FILES AND PROGRAMS

File sharing is an important part of any network. System 7 file sharing lets you designate up to ten folders or volumes on your computer to share with other computers on your network. You control who is permitted to use shared folders, as well as their specific access privileges.

In turn, you can access folders and volumes other Macintosh owners make available. Here's a brief summary of what file sharing lets you do:

▲ Use files stored on other computers.

▲ Let others share your files.

▲ Print documents on network printers.

▲ Update files across the network automatically. Information on this feature can be found in *Part V, The Finder.*

▲ Create links to an application on a remote computer. You can even link applications to exchange information, thus benefitting from the strengths of both. For example, a spreadsheet application

might ask a word-processing application to
spellcheck a worksheet.

A *network* is a combination of hardware and software
that lets computers communicate with each other. The
Macintosh comes with software for connecting it to
either an AppleTalk or LocalTalk network. All you need
to do is add the cables. Then you can share devices, such
as printers, with other network users.

If you have installed appropriate expansion cards, you
can connect to an AppleTalk network using EtherTalk or
TokenTalk software, which is included with System 7.

CONNECTING TO A NETWORK

If you have installed EtherTalk or TokenTalk software
and hardware, you can select that network connection.
Or, if you are connected to both a LocalTalk and an
Ethernet network, you can switch between them.

 PROCEDURE

To choose a network connection, follow these steps:

1. Open the *Apple* menu, open *Control Panels*, and
double-click to open the Network control panel.

The icons for any network connection software
you have installed display.

Network

2. Click the icon of the network connection you
   want. If you are using network services with your
   current network connection, you will be alerted
   that switching network connections will disconnect the current services. If this occurs, reconnect
   to the network services on the new network.

3. Click OK and close the Network control panel.

SELECTING A ZONE

Zones are set up by a network administrator to divide network devices into subgroups. If you are using a Token-
Talk or EtherTalk connection, you can choose a zone. If
you are on a LocalTalk network, skip this section.

Computers might be organized into zones by job function, location, or some other practical criterion.

PROCEDURE

To select a zone, follow these steps:

1. Choose *Control Panels* from the *Apple* menu and open the Network control panel.

2. Select the icon for the network connection you want.

3. Click the icon again. A list of available zone names displays in a dialog box.

4. Click to select a zone name from the list.

5. Click OK and close the Network control panel.

NOTE

AppleTalk is turned on for you when you connect to the network and turn on your Macintosh. If you wish to turn it off, select *Chooser* from the *Apple* menu and click the Inactive button. When you want to turn it back on, click the Active button and close the Chooser.

SHARING FILES AND PROGRAMS

195

TURNING ON FILE SHARING

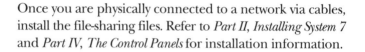

Once you are physically connected to a network via cables, install the file-sharing files. Refer to *Part II, Installing System 7* and *Part IV, The Control Panels* for installation information.

___ **PROCEDURE**

To turn file sharing on, follow these steps:

1. Choose *Control Panels* from the *Apple* menu. Double-click on the Sharing Setup control panel to open it.

Sharing Setup

The sharing setup dialog box appears, as shown in Figure VI.1.

2. Enter the name you want to use when accessing other computers in the Owner Name box. Up to 31 characters are allowed.

3. Press Tab. Enter your password in the Owner Password box. Up to eight characters are allowed. When you enter your password to connect to the network, you must match the password exactly, including the casing. You may change your password at any time by typing a new password in the Owner Password box and pressing Tab.

4. Press Tab. Enter a name for your Macintosh in the Macintosh Name box. This will represent your computer on the network.

5. Click the File Sharing Start button to turn file sharing on. File sharing remains on until you turn it off.

6. Close the Sharing Setup control panel.

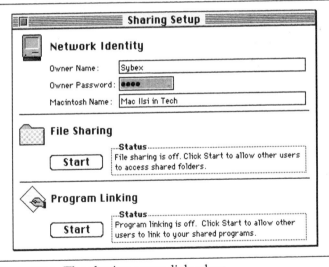

Figure VI.1: The sharing setup dialog box

PROCEDURE

To turn file sharing off, follow these steps:

1. Choose *Control Panels* from the *Apple* menu and double-click on the Sharing Setup control panel to open it. The sharing setup dialog box appears.

2. Click the File Sharing Stop button to turn file sharing off. (The Start button becomes the Stop button when file sharing is turned on.) A dialog box appears, as shown in Figure VI.2.

3. Enter the number of minutes you want to elapse before the network connection is terminated. You can enter a number between zero and 999. If, for

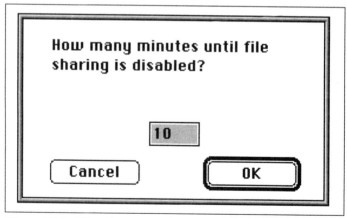

Figure VI.2: The disconnect dialog box

example, you specify a ten-minute delay before file sharing is turned off, users accessing your files are warned of the impending shutdown, giving them time to save their work.

 NOTE

If you select either the *Shut Down* or *Restart* command when network users are connected to your computer, an alert dialog box appears. It informs you there are people connected to your Mac and asks you to enter the number of minutes you will allow before file sharing shuts off. You might consider canceling the command to permit users to finish their work.

NAMING USERS

You specify who can access your folders and disks as well as their *access privileges*. Access privileges determine what remote users can do with a shared item. Although you can name as many as one hundred users and groups of users, it is recommended that you limit the number to under fifty. This section gives you information on naming users and assigning access privileges to them. A named user is referred to as a *registered user*.

You can specify access privileges for shared items whether or not you name specific users. See the section *Assigning Access Privileges* at the end of this part.

PROCEDURE

To name an individual user, follow these steps:

1. Choose *Control Panels* from the *Apple* menu and double-click on the Users & Groups control panel to open it.

Users & Groups

When the control panel opens you will see two icons. The bold icon represents you, the owner of the computer. The other is the Guest icon. You can use this icon to permit anyone on the network access to your computer.

2. Choose *New User* from the *File* menu. A New User icon appears.

New User

3. Type a name for the user. If you don't want to assign a password, skip to step 9.

4. Open the user icon by double-clicking it to assign a password. A window appears, as shown in Figure VI.3.

5. Type a password in the User Password box. It
can be up to eight characters in length. Make
sure to give each user his exact password, noting

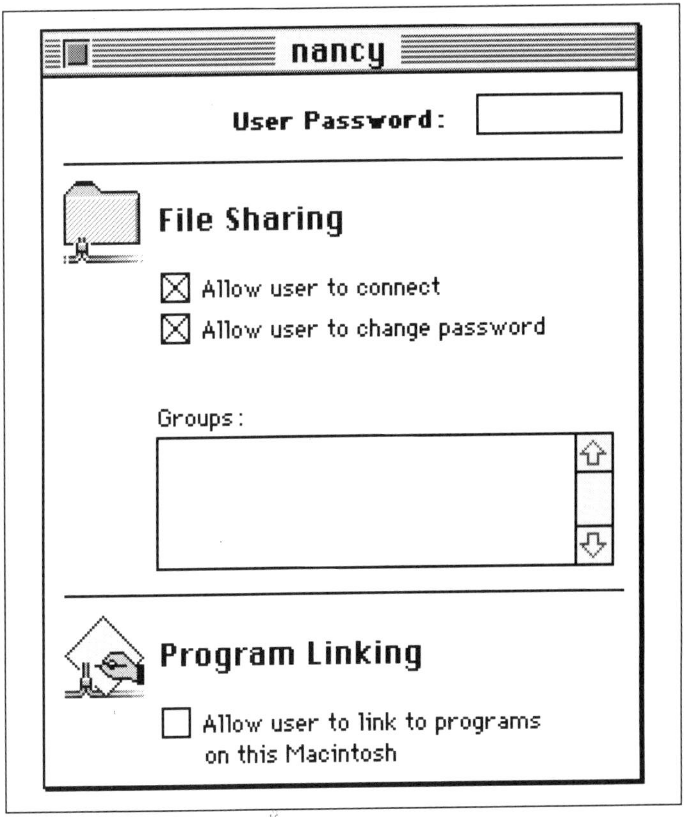

Figure VI.3: Entering a password

upper- and lowercase. (You can open a user
icon at any time and change the password.)

6. Press Tab. You can repeat steps 1 through 6 to add
other registered users. To delete a user, select his
icon and drag it to the Trash.

7. Check the *Allow user to connect* box if you want to
allow a user to connect to your computer from his
or her Mac.

8. Check the *Allow user to change password* box if you
want to allow the user to change his password
from his own computer.

9. Close the window and click Save in the dialog box.

10. Close the Users & Groups control panel.

KEYBOARD SHORTCUT

The Keyboard shortcut for New User is ⌘-**N**.

NOTE

You can deny guest access by choosing *Control Panels*
from the *Apple* menu and opening the Users & Groups
control panel. Double-click on the Guest icon to open it.
The <Guest> window is shown in Figure VI.4.

Click the box labeled *Allow guests to connect* to remove
the X. Close the window and click Save in the dialog box.

Naming Groups

If there is a group of people with similar work needs, it is easier to name a *group* of users rather than each individual user. A named group is referred to as a *registered group.*

 PROCEDURE

To name a group, follow these steps:

1. Choose *Control Panels* from the *Apple* menu and double-click the Users & Groups control panel.

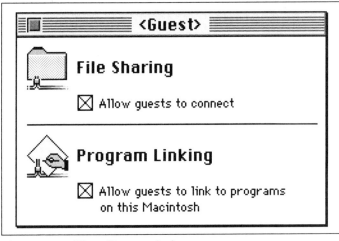

Figure VI.4: The <Guest> window

2. Choose *New Group* from the *File* menu. A new icon displays, labeled New Group.

New Group

3. Replace the icon's name with a name for the group. To delete the group, drag its icon to the Trash.

4. Drag the user icons of individuals you want to be members of the group to the new group's icon. To delete a user from a group, open the group's icon and drag the user's icon to the Trash.

5. Close the Users & Groups control panel.

NOTE

If you open the group icon, you will see a member icon for every user that you have added to the group.

Beth

If you open either a member icon (in the group icon window) or a user icon (in the Users & Groups control panel) you will see a list in the Groups box of the groups the user belongs to.

SHARING FOLDERS AND DISKS ▲

You can share up to ten folders, mounted volumes, hard disks, hard-disk partitions, CD-ROMs, or removable cartridges. Although you can share up to ten folders or disks at a time, this number doesn't include subfolders or folders stored on shared disks. You cannot share information on a floppy disk.

Before you can share folders or disks, you must turn on file sharing and assign a name to your Macintosh. Consider setting aside a folder or an entire hard disk as shared or public space.

 PROCEDURE

To designate the folder or disk you want to share, follow these steps:

1. Open the disk with the file or folder you want to share.

2. Click the folder or disk you want to share.

3. Choose *Sharing...* from the *File* menu. A dialog box appears, as shown in Figure VI.5.

4. Click the *Share this item and its contents* checkbox. If you want the status of the folder or disk returned

205

to private use, click on the checkbox to remove the *X.*

5. The *User/Group* pop-up menu displays the names of the users and groups that you named. You can choose one user or group from the list. The name you choose displays.

6. If the bottom row of checkboxes displays *Xs,* the shared item can be used by everyone on the network. To limit access to the chosen user or group, click the bottom row of three checkboxes to

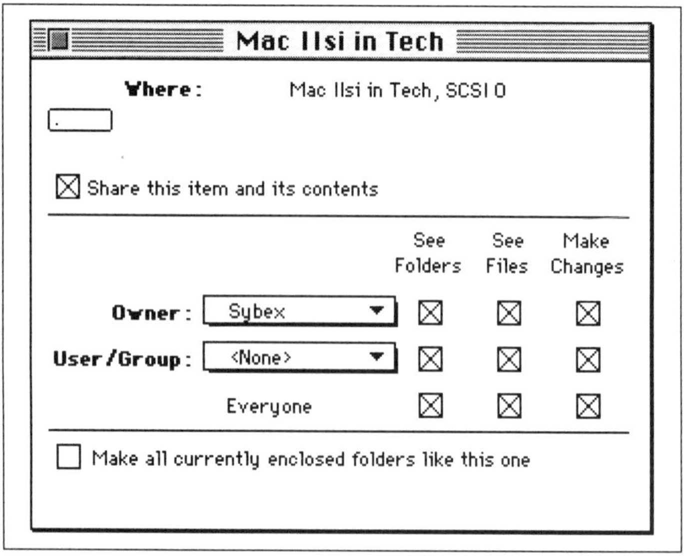

Figure VI.5: The file-sharing dialog box

remove the displayed *Xs*. You can further limit a user's access by deselecting the *See Folders*, *See Files*, and *Make Changes* checkboxes. See the section *Assigning Access Privileges* for more information on access privileges.

7. Close the window. When the save dialog box appears, click Save to change the sharing status. When a folder can be shared, the icon displays with network cables attached. When network users are connected to the folder or disk, the icon appears with faces on it.

8. Drag any files and folders you want to make available to network users into the shared folder.

MONITORING FILE SHARING

You can see the folders and disks you've shared and monitor who is connected to your Mac.

 PROCEDURE

To monitor file sharing, follow these steps:

1. Open *Control Panels* from the *Apple* menu. Double-click the File Sharing Monitor icon.

SHARING FILES AND PROGRAMS

File Sharing Monitor

The File Sharing Monitor window opens, as shown in Figure VI.6. You can see all shared folders and disks on your Mac on the left, in the Shared Items box. Any network users connected to your Mac display on the right in the Connected Users box. You can use the scroll bar to see more of the list. The bar at the bottom of the window shows the level of file sharing activity on your computer.

2. To disconnect a user from your Macintosh, select his name from the displayed list. To disconnect more than one user at a time, hold down Shift while clicking on user names.

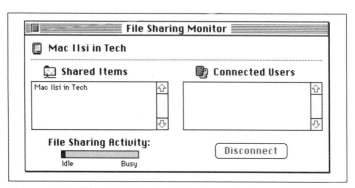

Figure VI.6: The File Sharing Monitor window

3. Click Disconnect.

4. Enter the number of minutes you want to elapse before the user is disconnected. Be sure to give people enough time to save their work!

5. Click OK and close the File Sharing Monitor window.

CONNECTING TO SHARED FOLDERS AND DEVICES

If you are going to access only items shared by other network users, you don't have to turn file sharing on. Before you try to connect to shared folders and devices, such as printers, on the network, find out:

▲ The name of the computer that has the shared disk you want to access.

▲ The name of the zone the computer is in.

▲ Whether you are a registered user on that computer. If you are registered, find out your user name and password.

▲ Whether the computer allows *guest access*. Guest access allows any network user to access the computer.

PROCEDURE

To connect to a shared item, follow these steps:

1. Select *Chooser* from the *Apple* menu. Make sure that AppleTalk is active.

2. Click the AppleShare icon in the upper-left section of the Chooser window.

3. If your network is divided into zones, click the name of the zone you want. The list of zones displays in a box on the lower-left side. If your network has many zones, you might have to scroll to see the one you want. When you select a zone, the available devices (other Macs, printers, file servers, and so on) in that zone display in the upper-right section of the Chooser window. If the network is *not* divided into zones, you will not see a list.

4. Click the name of the computer you want from the box on the right side of the window. (The Mac refers to *all* computers as *File Servers.*) Figure VI.7 displays one available disk.

5. Click the OK button and a dialog box appears. You can access the folder as a guest or as a registered user. Click the button that gives you the access you want. If you click Guest, skip to step 8 below.

6. Type your registered user's name. Uppercase and lowercase letters do not have to match.

7. Type your password exactly as it is registered, including upper- and lowercase letters.

8. Click OK. A list of shared items displays in a dialog box. See Figure VI.8.

9. Select the names of the items you want to access.

10. To connect to a shared disk automatically at startup, click the checkbox next to its name. (If you are connecting as a guest, you won't have this option, so skip the next step.)

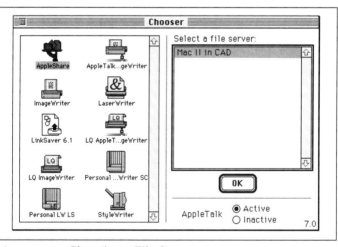

Figure VI.7: Choosing a File Server

SHARING FILES AND PROGRAMS

11. Click *Save My Name Only* to enter a password and access the shared item. Click *Save My Name and Password* to connect automatically. Note, though, that the latter is a *less secure method*.

12. Click OK and close the Chooser window. The shared-folder icon displays on your screen. You can use any of the files in this folder as if they were on your hard disk, depending on your access privileges.

13. Double-click on the folder to open it. If you edit the documents within the folder, when you save

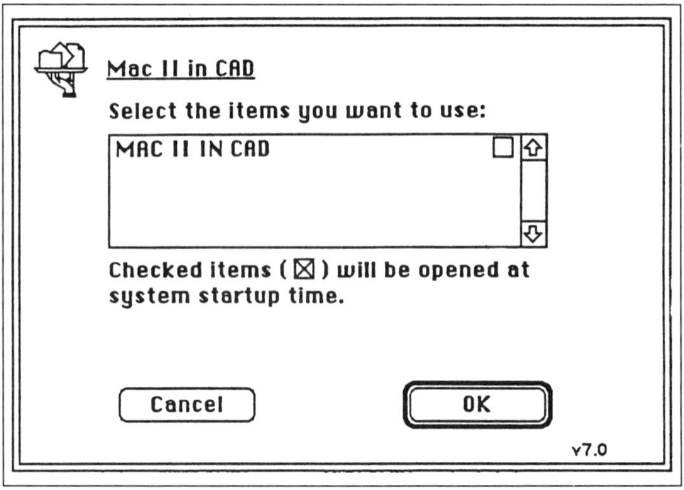

Figure VI.8: The shared items dialog box

your changes, the revised document will replace the original one on the network. If you create a new folder, you become the folder's owner. See the section *Understanding Folder Ownership*.

Changing Your Password

 PROCEDURE

To change the password you use to connect to your own computer from a remote computer, follow these steps:

1. Choose *Control Panels* from the *Apple* menu and open the Sharing Setup control panel.

2. Type a new password in the Owner Password box.

3. Press Tab. The characters of your password are replaced by bullets to keep them private.

4. Close the Sharing Setup control panel.

Registered users can sometimes change their passwords. The shared item's owner grants this privilege by selecting *Allow user to change password* when naming users.

PROCEDURE

To change your password, follow these steps:

1. Follow steps 1 through 5 under the section *To connect to a shared item.* A dialog box displays.

2. Click the Set Password button.

3. Enter your current password.

4. Press Tab and enter a new password.

5. Click OK. A dialog box appears telling you to retype your new password. Click OK.

6. Retype your password and click OK.

 PROCEDURE

To disconnect from a shared item, close all files of the shared item. Then, select the item's icon and either drag it to the Trash or choose *Put Away* from the *File* menu. Another way to disconnect from shared items is to shut down your Mac!

Understanding Folder Ownership

Ownership permits you to set access privileges for an item. If you create a folder on a remote Mac, you become the folder's owner, and only you can change its access privileges. Folders that you own display a tabbed-folder icon.

Games

Note that you will see the tab only if you are viewing files *by Icon.*

You can also create a folder inside another network user's folder. The parent folder continues to be owned by the original owner. You own only the enclosed folder you have created.

You can even give ownership to someone else who can restrict your access! Since the new owner can deny you access to your own materials, proceed cautiously.

PROCEDURE

To transfer ownership, follow these steps:

1. Select a folder you own. It can be on your disk or on a remote disk.

2. Choose *Sharing...* from the *File* menu.

3. You can transfer ownership only to a registered user or group. Use the pop-up menu to select a new owner or select the Owner box and type the name of a user or group.

4. Close the dialog box. You will be asked to confirm the access changes. Click Save.

 PROCEDURE

To connect to another computer automatically, follow these steps:

1. Connect to a shared item following the steps in the section *Connecting to Shared Folders and Devices.*

2. Select the shared item and choose *Make Alias* from the *File* menu.

3. Put the alias in a convenient place.

4. Close all files and disconnect from the shared item by dragging its icon to the Trash.

5. Double-click the alias the next time you want to use the shared disk. If you originally connected to the shared item as a registered user, a password dialog box appears. Type your password. The shared disk's icon will appear on your screen.

PROCEDURE

To prevent your computer from automatically connecting on startup, follow these steps:

1. Select *Chooser* from the *Apple* menu.

2. Click the AppleShare icon in the Chooser window.

3. Click the name of the shared item you are connected to.

4. Click OK.

5. Click Guest or Registered User.

6. If you are a registered user, check the displayed name to make sure it is correct. Make changes if it isn't.

7. Type your password and click OK.

8. Deselect the checkbox alongside the shared item.

9. Click OK and close the Chooser.

ACCESSING YOUR MAC REMOTELY

You can access your computer from another computer on the network, provided your computer is turned on and file sharing is on. This is especially useful if you are working on a remote Mac.

 PROCEDURE

To access your Mac from another computer, follow these steps:

1. Choose *Control Panels* from the *Apple* menu and double-click on the Users & Groups control panel to open it.

2. The Owner icon appears with a bold outline. Open it.

Sybex

3. To see and use materials on another computer's hard disk, click the boxes labeled *Allow user to connect* and *Allow user to see entire disk.* If you do not want to access anything on your own computer from another computer, remove the *X* from the *Allow user to see entire disk* box.

4. Close the window and the Users & Groups control panel.

5. Connect to your computer as a registered user, entering your name and password.

6. Continue connecting as usual.

ASSIGNING ACCESS PRIVILEGES ▲

You might have set access privileges when you originally shared the folder or disk. If you want to change the privileges you originally set, read the following.

PROCEDURE

To set access privileges for your shared items, select the item and choose the *Sharing...* command from the *File* menu. The window shown in Figure VI.9 appears, offering you options for setting access privileges.

Setting Access Privileges

You control the access to your shared items by specifying who can use the item and in what way. When you share files, there are many strategies you can use to create the security you need on your Mac. As the shared item's owner, you use the window shown in Figure VI.8 to check options, selecting the particular combination of check-boxes you want.

219

You can use this window to set access privileges for three levels of user.

▲ The *Owner* box is a pop-up menu that displays your name, <Any User>, and any registered users. You automatically become the owner of a folder when you create it. You can transfer ownership to a registered user or group. To allow anyone on the network to modify the folder's access privileges, select <Any User>.

▲ The *User/Group* box is a pop-up menu that displays a list of registered users and groups or <None>. You can select a user or group name from the list.

		See Folders	See Files	Make Changes
	MAC II IN CAD			
Where:	MAC II IN CAD, Mac II in CAD			
Connected As:	nancy			
Privileges:	See Folders, See Files, Make Changes			
Owner:	nancy	☒	☒	☒
User/Group:		☐	☐	☐
	Everyone	☐	☐	☐
☐ Make all currently enclosed folders like this one				

Figure VI.9: The access priveleges window

▲ *Everyone* refers to all network users and guests.

There are three kinds of access privilege. You can assign a particular kind of access privilege for each of the previous users or groups by checking any of the following boxes alongside their names.

▲ *See Folders* lets users view folders within a folder or disk. Users can open and copy these folders. If you don't check this option, these folders do not display.

▲ *See Files* lets users open a folder, view the folder's contents, and copy them to their own disks. If you don't check this option, files within a shared item do not display.

▲ *Make Changes* lets users save new files to a folder. When *See Folders* and *See Files* are also checked, users can open, copy, rename, change, or delete files or folders within the folder.

There are two checkboxes at the bottom of the window.

▲ *Make all currently enclosed folders like this one* assigns the privileges of the current folder to any enclosed folders. If you are sharing a folder for the first time, this option is not necessary since every new folder is automatically set to the same privileges as the enclosing folder. You can set specific privileges separately if you like.

▲ The *Can't be moved, renamed or deleted* checkbox locks the folder so its name and location can't be changed. This is a good security option.

NOTE

If you select a folder that is inside a shared folder, and choose *Sharing...* from the *File* menu, you see another checkbox. Checking the *Same as enclosing folder* checkbox forces the folder to adopt the privileges of the enclosing folder. This means that moving the folder to a new parent folder with different access privileges causes the enclosed folder's access privileges to change to those of the new parent folder.

Understanding File Sharing Icons

Table VI.1 shows the file-sharing icons you might see.

When you open a shared item on another computer, you can see icons on the left side of the space below the window's title bar. These icons show you only what you *cannot* do. (If you have complete access privileges, you will not see any icons.)

The pencil icon means *no changes*.

The folder icon means *can't see folders*.

The document icon means *can't see files*.

Table VI.1: File Sharing Icons

	Network cables attached to a folder indicate the folder is a shared item.
	A tabbed folder indicates that you are the owner of the folder.
	A belted folder indicates you cannot open it.
	A belted folder with an arrow indicates you cannot open the folder but you can save items to it. This type of folder is referred to as a *drop box*. A drop box must be a folder within a shared folder and disk.
	A folder with faces on it indicates a network user is currently accessing it.

LINKING APPLICATIONS

Some applications can communicate and exchange information directly with other applications. If the applications have this capability, you can link them across a network and allow other network users to link their applications to yours. You control whether or not network users can link to your applications in the following ways:

▲ No one can link to applications on your computer until you turn on program linking.

▲ No one can link to applications of yours unless you specifically make them available.

▲ You determine which network users can link to the applications you have made available.

Linking to Remote Applications

For users to link to a network application, the owner must first share the program. Check the application's documentation for information about how it implements linking.

 PROCEDURE

To link to an application program on a remote computer, follow these steps:

1. Choose the menu item that lets you link from within the application. Select the Macintosh you want to connect to. (If your network has zones, select the zone as well.)

2. Select the application you want to link to. Click OK.

3. Click Guest or Registered User. If you are a registered user, check the displayed name to make sure it is correct. If it isn't, correct it.

4. Type your password and click OK.

Quitting the application from which you created the link disconnects the link.

Letting Users Link to Your Applications

You can let network users create links between their applications and yours. To do this, AppleTalk must be active in the Chooser and you must have named your Macintosh as described in the section *Turning File Sharing On*.

 PROCEDURE

To let network users link to your application, follow these steps:

1. Choose *Control Panels* from the *Apple* menu and double-click on the Sharing Setup control panel.

225

2. Click the Start button located in the bottom section of the window. Application linking starts up and the button changes to Stop.

3. Close the control panel.

4. Select the application you want to share. (Check its documentation to make sure it has this capability.)

5. Choose *Sharing...* from the *File* menu.

6. Check the box labeled *Allow remote program linking*. If the checkbox is dimmed, the application you have selected does not permit linking.

7. Close the window. Network users can link their applications to this application as long as your computer is turned on, linking is turned on, and the application is running.

Naming Users to Link to Applications

You can specify the network users you want to allow to link to your applications. First, you must name them on your computer, as described in the sections *Naming Users* and *Naming Groups*.

PROCEDURE

To specify network users, follow these steps:

1. Choose *Control Panels* from the *Apple* menu and open the Users & Groups control panel.

2. Double-click on the user icon to open it. To allow everyone on the network to link to your shared application, select the Guest icon.

3. Check the *Allow user to link to programs on this Macintosh* checkbox.

4. Close the window and click Save in the dialog box. Repeat steps 2 through 4 to name other users.

NOTE

To remove a registered user or group, drag the icon to the Trash. The users will no longer be able to link their applications to yours.

227

INDEX

FILE MENU SHORTCUTS

▲

Keyboard Shortcut	Action
⌘-N	Creates a new folder
⌘-O	Opens selected item
⌘-P	Prints files from the Finder
⌘-W	Closes window
⌘-I	*Get Info* command
⌘-D	Duplicates item
⌘-Y	Returns item to its original place or ejects disk
⌘-F	*Find…* command
⌘-G	*Find Again* command